IS IT A CHOICE?

D0974228

ALSO BY ERIC MARCUS

The Male Couple's Guide: Finding a Man, Making
    a Home, Building a Life
Making History: The Struggle for Gay and Lesbian
    Equal Rights, 1945–1990
Expect the Worst (You Won't Be Disappointed)
Breaking the Surface, with Greg Louganis
Why Suicide? Answers to 200 of the Most
    Frequently Asked Questions About Suicide,
    Attempted Suicide, and Assisted Suicide
Icebreaker: The Autobiography of Rudy Galindo,
    with Rudy Galindo
Together Forever: Gay and Lesbian Couples Share
    Their Secrets for Lasting Happiness

❯ **Please visit my Web site at www.ericmarcus.com**

IS IT A
CHOICE

Answers to 300 of the Most
Frequently Asked Questions
About Gay and Lesbian People

?

Eric Marcus

 HarperSanFrancisco
A Division of HarperCollins*Publishers*

MONTROSE LIBRARY DISTRICT
320 So. 2nd St.
Montrose, CO 81401

> To Duf, who wasn't afraid to ask.

IS IT A CHOICE?: *Answers to 300 of the Most Frequently Asked Questions About Gay and Lesbian People.* Copyright © 1999 by Eric Marcus. All rights reserved. Printed in the United States of America. No part of this book may be used or reproduced in any manner whatsoever without written permission except in the case of brief quotations embodied in critical articles and reviews. For information address HarperCollins Publishers, 10 East 53rd Street, New York, NY 10022.

HarperCollins books may be purchased for educational, business, or sales promotional use. For information please write: Special Markets Department, HarperCollins Publishers, Inc., 10 East 53rd Street, New York, NY 10022.

HarperCollins Web Site: http://www.harpercollins.com
HarperCollins®, 📖®, and HarperSanFrancisco™ are trademarks of HarperCollins Publishers Inc.

SECOND EDITION

FIRST HARPERSANFRANCISCO EDITION PUBLISHED 1993

Library of Congress Cataloging-in-Publication Data
Marcus, Eric.
Is it a choice?: answers to 300 of the most frequently asked
questions about gay and lesbian people / Eric Marcus. —2nd ed.
Includes bibliographical references and index.
ISBN 0–06–251623–X (pbk.)
1. Homosexuality—United States—Miscellanea. 2. Gay men—
United States—Miscellanea. 3. Lesbians—United States—
Miscellanea.
I. Title.
HQ76.3.U5M35   1999   99–17799

305.9'0664—dc21
                  02 03 RRD(H)   20 19 18 17 16 15 14 13 12 11

MONTROSE LIBRARY DISTRICT
320 So. 2nd St.
Montrose, CO 81401

CONTENTS

ACKNOWLEDGMENTS

Many thanks to my editor, Barbara Moulton, for sharing my enthusiasm for *Is It a Choice?*; to Alison Ames, for generously providing a very comfortable place to work; to Barry Owen, for his help on the proposal; and to Ann Northrop, for her wisdom, encouragement, and support. And special thanks to all those who suggested questions, offered sage advice, and/or read the manuscript, including Lisa Bach, Dr. Betty Berzon, Mark Burstein, Cate Corcoran, Christine Egan, Ilan Greenberg, Cynthia Grossman, Fred Hertz's grandmother, Alex Lash, Aaron Levaco, Peggy Levine, Matthew Lore, Cecilia Marcus, Steven Mazzola, Bill Megevick, Judy Montague, Jessica Morris, Joel Roselin, Phil Roselin, Bill Russell, Stuart Schear, Bill Smith, Scott Terranella, and Nick Wingfield.

For the second edition, many thanks to my editor, Liz Perle, and her eagle-eyed assistant, David Hennessy, for their unwavering support and help. Thank you also to my researchers, Jennifer Finlay and Stephen Milioti, for making certain that this latest edition of *Is It a Choice?* contains the most current and accurate information available. Thank you Nancy Kokolj for reviewing the finished manuscript. A special thank you to my meticulous copyeditor, Carl Walesa. And, as always, thank you to my H. B., Barney Karpfinger, for so much.

INTRODUCTION

Not long ago, while on a flight from New York City to Syracuse, New York, the passenger sitting to my right asked me where I was headed. I said that I was going to the State University in Oswego to give a talk. "About what?" she asked. I wished she hadn't asked, because given past experience I knew that you could never be too sure who was sitting next to you no matter how benign they might look. But, figuring we were at the tail end of our short flight, I felt confident that if I told her about my talk we wouldn't get into any major trouble in the time we had left before landing.

I explained to my seatmate that my talk was about how difficult it is for gay and lesbian people to keep their lives secret and why it was important for those of us who can be honest about our sexual orientation to live openly. My seatmate then identified herself as a born-again Christian. Recalling a recent encounter on another flight with a woman who was a member of Focus on the Family, a conservative religious organization that spreads antigay propaganda and actively opposes equal rights for gay and lesbian people, my heart sank.

Religious fundamentalists, especially those affiliated with conservative right-wing political organizations, generally have fixed—and negative—ideas about homosexuality. The woman from Focus on the Family suggested that I might want to take one of their courses on how to "come out of the homosexual lifestyle." Without trying to explain that homosexuality was not a lifestyle and without asking her if she had ever considered taking a course on becoming a lesbian, I firmly declined the offer.

So, given past experience, after my Syracuse-bound seatmate told me about her religious background, I didn't have much in the way of hope for where the conversation was likely to go. But, as I often do, I had judged too quickly. My seatmate had a number of sincere, although difficult to answer, questions about religious faith and homosexuality. For starters, she wanted to know how gay and lesbian people could "reconcile their actions with the word of God as expressed in the Bible." There wasn't nearly enough time to adequately discuss something so complex, and I'm hardly an expert on Christianity, but I made my best effort in the few minutes we had.

I've been answering questions about homosexuality for what feels like a very long time. But it wasn't until 1988, when my first book—*The Male Couple's Guide*—was published that I realized just how little most people knew about homosexuality. During the ten-day media tour that took me across the country, I never got to talk about couple relationships because all the questions directed at me had to do with basic issues, such as "How do you know you're a homosexual?" "How do parents react to a gay child?" "Why do gay people want to get married?" "Do gay parents raise gay children?" "Who plays the husband and who plays the wife?" "Why do gay people have to flaunt it?" And, of course, there was the occasional caller on the live radio talk shows who insisted on telling me that God created Adam and Eve, not Adam and Steve.

What really drove home the point to me that there was a desperate need for clear, concise answers about gay and lesbian people and the lives we lead came at the end of the tour, during dinner with my good friends Duffie and Simeon. I was feeling very frustrated about my experiences on the road and told them: "You can't believe the stupid questions I have to answer." Duf asked, "What kinds of stupid questions do people ask you?" And I gave a long list of the kinds of things people asked, including the question asked most frequently, "Is it a choice?" Duf flushed, paused, and said, "Those don't sound like stupid questions to me." Simeon said, "Isn't it a choice?" I almost fell off my chair. These were my friends. Didn't they know? After all, they had known me for five years, since Duf and I had met at graduate school. The fact I was gay had never been an issue. But I realized that we had never really talked about it after the first time I told Duf I was gay. I just assumed they already had the answers.

The next week, I had dinner with mutual friends, Kate and Rick. They're a little older than Duffie and Simeon and I simply assumed they'd be as shocked as I was at how little Duffie and Simeon knew about gay people. So I related what happened the week before. I got to the point in the story where Duf commented, "Those don't sound like stupid questions," and Kate asked me, "What kinds of questions are people asking?" I told her and she said, "Those don't sound like stupid questions to me." Again, I was shocked. Even my own friends knew very little about gay men and lesbians.

After that night, I was determined to write a book that included all the questions I had ever been asked and then some. The problem I quickly discovered, though, was finding a publishing company that thought such a book was necessary. Despite the many rejections, I didn't give up, and five years after that dinner with Duffie and Simeon, Is It A Choice? was published. And now, six years and fifty thousand copies later, it's time to publish a new, updated edition of Is It A Choice?

A lot has changed for gay and lesbian people since the first edition of Is It A Choice? went on sale in 1993. And a lot hasn't. First the changes, both the good and the bad.

Two 1993 front-burner issues, AIDS and "gays in the military" are no longer at the center of discussion. The battle over gays in the military was resolved when the Congress and President Bill Clinton agreed to the Don't Ask, Don't Tell, Don't Pursue policy. The President's objective, to make it easier for gay people to serve in the military, didn't turn out as expected. More gay and lesbian service people have been tossed out of the military since "Don't Ask, Don't Tell," was put in place than before. According to Pentagon officials, discharges increased to 1,145 in 1998, up from 997 the year before. This was the fifth consecutive annual rise.

AIDS remains a major concern, but with the advent of new drugs to treat the disease and a subsequent dramatic drop in the death rate, AIDS is no longer the acute crisis for gay men that it once was. Along with the good news, there is rising concern over the alarming increase in the HIV infection rate among young gay men—African American and Hispanic men in particular—and the growing disregard for safer sex practices.

Since 1993, gay marriage has moved front and center as one of the key issues of the gay civil rights struggle. Gay and lesbian people across the country have taken up the fight for legal marriage, which has led to high-profile court cases, state referenda, anti-gay marriage state and federal legislation, public protests, and heated debates, both public and private. While western European countries have moved in the direction of giving gay and lesbian couples the same or similar rights and privileges granted heterosexual married couples, the outcome of the gay marriage debate in the United States is at best uncertain. What is certain, however, is that the ongoing debate will be a heated one and the issue will be with us for years to come.

Whatever the outcome of the gay marriage fight, small companies and large corporations alike now provide benefits to the domestic partners of gay and lesbian employees. And due in large part to the efforts of gay and lesbian employees and increasingly powerful gay and lesbian employee groups within major corporations, the number of businesses offering such benefits continues to grow at a rapid pace.

Over the past six years, national and local gay and lesbian organizations have continued to grow in numbers and strength. Most encouraging, in my mind, has been the dramatic increase in the number of gay/straight alliances for gay and lesbian high school students and their supportive non-gay friends. These gay/straight alliances have grown from just a handful in the early 1990s to approximately 500 by 1999 at schools across the nation.

One dramatic change that has helped fuel the formation of new organizations and the growth of older ones has been the Internet. The Internet has given gay and lesbian people, many of whom are often isolated, a direct connection to each other and the organized gay community. Gay and lesbian people, no matter where they live, and no matter how deeply hidden they are, can now find information and friendship on an astonishing array of Web sites.

Public perception of gay people and opinions heterosexuals have about us and the issues that affect our lives have continued to move in a positive direction as they have since the 1970s. While gay and lesbian people remain one of the most disliked groups in the nation, we're not disliked nearly as much as we once were. Only a slight majority of Americans now disapprove of homosexuality, and a significant majority supports the right of gay men and women to equal opportunities in employment. And despite a ban on openly gay people serving in the military, 66 percent of the American public supports the inclusion of gay and lesbian people in the military. But there is still a long way to go regarding the attitudes of Americans toward gay and lesbian people. A 1998 *Newsweek* poll found that 56 percent of repondents believe that gay men and lesbians "can change their sexual orientation through therapy, will power, or religious conviction." Only 33 percent "approve of legally sanctioned gay marriage." And only 36 percent believe gay men and women "should be allowed to adopt children."

On the political/legal front, there have been a number of high-profile victories. In 1998, Dade County, Florida, which repealed its gay rights ordinance in 1977, following an anti-gay campaign led by entertainer Anita Bryant, passed a new gay rights ordinance. Also in 1998, Georgia's high court voided that state's anti-sodomy law, twelve years after the U.S. Supreme Court upheld Georgia's anti-sodomy statute in a landmark decision. Georgia's own Supreme Court invalidated the law by ruling that private consensual sodomy between adults is protected under privacy rights guaranteed by the State Constitution. And in New Jersey, a male couple sued that state for the right to jointly adopt their foster child. In winning their case, they became the first gay or lesbian couple to be allowed to jointly adopt a child. (Prior to this case, such an adoption would have required two separate, and costly adoption procedures.)

What hasn't changed in the past six years is the hatred and violence expressed toward gay and lesbian people from young thugs who seek out gay men and women as targets for beatings and worse to religious and political leaders who think nothing of inflaming anti-gay sentiment through their public statements of bigotry and ignorance. And despite how much the public has been exposed to gay and lesbian issues through their favorite television programs, as well as discussions with gay and lesbian loved ones around the dinner table, most people remain woefully ignorant about gay and lesbian people and the lives we lead. In addition, young gay and lesbian people continue to search for answers to the many questions they have about themselves and the lives they can hope to lead. This is why there is as great a need today for *Is It A Choice?* as there was in 1993.

There may very well come a day when *Is It a Choice?* is no longer needed; I look forward to that time. But as long as gay and lesbian young people grow up in fear of their own parents and national political leaders think nothing of making ignorant statements about gay and lesbian Americans, that day will remain far, far in the future. Until that time comes, I hope the questions and answers on these pages continue to bring needed light to a subject that remains clouded by ignorance and destructive myths.

The questions and answers you'll find in *Is It a Choice?* come from many different sources. Most of the questions are my own, while others were gathered from friends, family, and perfect strangers. For the answers to the more than three hundred questions included here, I talked to many people—including experts from a variety of fields. In addition to depending on magazine and newspaper articles, I also read through scores of books. My responses range from exceedingly brief to detailed and involved. You'll find plenty of anecdotes, opinions, and conjecture, and more than a few of the questions will leave you with more questions, because I've included questions that don't yet have definitive answers.

The answers I offer here are not the only possible ones to the questions I pose. Other gay and lesbian people would likely answer these questions differently because gay men and women are a diverse population with different values and different ways of looking at our world.

Some people will be disappointed to discover in the answers I offer that gay and lesbian people aren't nearly as exotic as we've sometimes been portrayed, especially by those groups that would have you believe we are forever parading, scantily clad in black leather or sequins, down the main streets of the nation's cities. In fact, some gay and lesbian people *are* pretty exotic, as are some heterosexual people (have you ever been to Mardi Gras?). But in writing a general question-and-answer book like *Is It a Choice?* I stuck pretty close to the broad middle of lesbian and gay life.

You'll meet all kinds of people in *Is It a Choice?* Some give answers to questions; others provide stories that help support a point. When I've used quotes or anecdotes from experts and public people, like gay and lesbian rights activists, I've used complete names. When I've quoted private citizens or used their anecdotes—some of which are composites drawn from several people—I've used only first names to protect the privacy of the people I'm quoting.

Is It a Choice? includes more than three hundred questions; but not all the possible questions about homosexuality are here, nor are all the answers. If there's a question I've missed that you'd like answered, or if you have an answer to a question that I either didn't have an answer for or that you feel I didn't answer adequately, write to me in care of my publisher or contact me via my Web page. And remember, there really is no such thing as a stupid question—except for the question that you don't ask.

Eric Marcus
c/o Harper San Francisco
353 Sacramento Street, Suite 500
San Francisco, CA 94111–3653
www.ericmarcus.com

1

?

THE BASICS

> ### What is a homosexual?

A homosexual person is a man or woman whose feelings of sexual attraction are for someone of the same sex. The word *homosexual* was first used by Karl Maria Kertbeny in an 1869 pamphlet in which he argued for the repeal of Prussia's antihomosexual laws. *Homosexual* combines the Greek word for "same" with the Latin word for "sex." In contrast, a heterosexual is a man or woman whose feelings of sexual attraction are for the opposite gender.

Homosexual people come in all shapes and sizes and from all walks of life, just like heterosexual people do. Some are single, and some are involved in long-term, loving relationships with same-gender partners. Some have children and grandchildren; others don't. Homosexual people are a part of every community and every family, which means that everyone knows someone who is homosexual. Most people just don't realize that they know, and perhaps love, someone who is homosexual, because many—if not most—homosexual people keep their sexual orientation a secret.

I wish I had known what a homosexual was when I was growing up. At first I didn't know exactly what a homosexual was, except that they were very bad and disgusting men who did terrible things to children—the kind of people your parents always told you not to accept candy from.

As I grew into adolescence, I still wasn't exactly sure what a homosexual was, never having actually met one, but I knew that the most horrible thing you could call someone was a "faggot." In summer camp, there was always at least one boy who got tagged with that label. It was usually someone who couldn't throw a ball and always struck out at baseball—a total wimp, despised by the other boys and shunned by the girls. One summer, I was that boy, and while I didn't really think of being a faggot in terms of wanting to have sex with other boys, I knew there was some truth in what they were calling me. Would I, I wondered, grow up to be one of those terrible men?

When I finally met someone I knew was a homosexual, I was so relieved. Bob was a smart, handsome, and very confident college student who lived down the block. He didn't lurk behind shrubs, and he never once offered me candy. He did, however, help dispel all the myths I had grown up with about homosexuals and homosexuality. He was the first person to explain to me that a homosexual is simply a man or woman whose feelings of sexual attraction are for someone of the same gender. One man could meet and fall in love with another man, my new friend explained, and one woman could fall in love with another woman. So simple, but to me it was a revolutionary idea and it changed my life.

❯ *What is a lesbian?*

A lesbian is a homosexual woman. The word derives from the name of a Greek island, Lesbos, where Sappho, a teacher known for her poetry celebrating love between women, established a school for young women in the sixth century B.C. Over time, the word *lesbian*, which once simply meant someone who lived on Lesbos, came to mean a woman who, like Sappho and her followers, loved other women.

❯ *What is a gay person?*

Gay is a synonym for *homosexual*. Since the late 1960s, the word *gay* has been publicly adopted by homosexual men and women as a positive alternative to the clinical-sounding *homosexual*. *Gay* was used as slang in place of *homosexual* as far back as the 1920s, almost exclusively within the homosexual subculture. For example, when Lisa Ben published a newsletter for lesbians called *Vice Versa* back in 1947, she gave it the tag line "America's Gayest Magazine." Other homosexual people knew Lisa didn't mean that her magazine was simply full of fun. When Lisa spoke about herself or other lesbians, she used the phrase "gay gal." And she described places in Los Angeles where she and her friends were welcome as being popular with a "gay crowd."

Not all homosexual people like the word *gay*; some prefer the word *homosexual* to *gay*. And since *gay* has come to be used primarily in association with male homosexuals, many, if not most, homosexual women prefer to be called lesbians.

❯ *What is a bisexual?*

A bisexual person has significant feelings of sexual attraction for both men and women. These feelings may be stronger for the same gender or for the opposite gender. That simply depends on the individual.

Some people are under the mistaken impression that people who are bisexual are conducting relationships with both men and women at the same time. While this may be the case for some people, most bisexual men and women who are in relationships have only a single partner at a time.

› Aren't bisexuals people who are afraid to admit they're gay?

Some gay and lesbian people, as they deal with accepting their feelings, may first assert that they are bisexual. That's what I did. In my last year of high school I confided to a close male friend—who I thought might be gay—that I was bisexual. By this time I already knew I was gay because I had an overwhelming adolescent crush on Bob, the college student who lived down the block, and I wasn't the least bit interested in having a physical relationship with a woman. But somehow, "bisexual" didn't sound nearly as bad as "gay." If I said I was bisexual, I rationalized, at least I was half heterosexual. I could put one foot in the gay world and keep the other safely in the nongay world—in word, if not in deed. I imagined that people would have an easier time accepting me if they thought I went both ways. But within a couple of years, when I felt more comfortable about being gay, I gave up claiming that I was bisexual.

Unfortunately, because plenty of gay and lesbian people call themselves bisexual on the way to accepting their homosexual orientation, many people have the misconception that all men and women who say they are bisexual are homosexuals who are afraid to admit the truth about themselves. This is simply a misconception. There are many people who have feelings of sexual attraction for both men and women.

› What is the Kinsey scale?

Alfred Kinsey, whose landmark studies in the 1940s and 1950s on male and female sexuality first revealed the rich variety of human sexual expression, developed a seven-point rating scale to represent human sexual attraction. The Kinsey scale has a range of zero to six. The zero category includes all people who are exclusively heterosexual and report no homosexual experience or attraction. Category six includes those who are exclusively homosexual in experience and attraction. Everyone else falls somewhere in between.

> **How do you know if you're gay or lesbian?**

The key to knowing whether you're heterosexual, homosexual, or bisexual is to pay attention to your feelings of attraction. The challenge for many gay, lesbian, and bisexual people is being honest with themselves about what they're feeling, because society is, in general, so unaccepting of them.

One of the big challenges I faced in college as I began telling friends that I was gay was explaining to them how I knew I was gay. They wanted to know how I knew, which seemed reasonable. A quick way of responding to that question was to ask them how they knew they were heterosexual. They would usually answer that they had never thought about it or that they just knew. For example, they responded by telling me that for as long as they could remember, they found members of the opposite gender attractive. And I would respond by telling them that, substituting "same gender" for "opposite gender," it was the same for me.

Beyond that explanation, I usually tried to find an example my friends could relate to. One of the first people to ask me this question was my friend Cindy. The question happened to come up on a trip we made to New York City to see a ballet performance during our junior year of college. I decided to use the ballet as an example of how I knew I was gay. During intermission, I asked Cindy what she thought about the principal woman dancer. Cindy said that she was an excellent performer and very beautiful. I told her that I felt the same way. Then I asked her what she thought of the male dancer who performed a solo just before intermission. I knew Cindy well enough to know what her answer would be: "Oh my God, he's gorgeous! He's so sexy!" I told her that I felt the same way.

Mr. Gorgeous Dancer left us both breathless, and overwhelmed with desire. Using that example, I was able to convey to my friend that the experience of being attracted to someone—a man, in this case—was no different for me or for her. It was an experience so automatic that we didn't even have a chance to think about it before being overwhelmed by a quickening pulse. The difference, of course, was that almost everyone would consider her feelings for the dancer perfectly normal.

> **Can you be a gay man or a lesbian without ever having a sexual experience or relationship with someone of the same gender?**

Sexual orientation—homosexual, heterosexual, or bisexual—has everything to do with feelings of attraction and nothing to do with actual sexual experience. As you grow through childhood, you become aware of your feelings of attraction. That awareness, whether it's of attraction to the same gender, the opposite gender, or both genders, does not require actual physical experience. If you think back to your own early awareness of your attractions, more likely than not you knew whether you were attracted to members of the same gender, the opposite gender, or both long before becoming sexually active.

> **Can you have feelings of same-gender attraction and not be a homosexual?**
> **Can you have feelings of opposite-gender attraction and not be a heterosexual?**

Human sexuality is profoundly complex and not easily compartmentalized into rigid categories (as exemplified by the

Kinsey scale). So it should surprise no one that it's perfectly normal for a homosexual person to have feelings of attraction for someone of the opposite gender, just as it's perfectly normal for a heterosexual person to have feelings of attraction for someone of the same gender.

However, even though these feelings are something almost all people experience at one time or another in their lives, they can still be very confusing. For example, the first time I had an erotic dream about a woman, I was probably nineteen or twenty. I woke up in the morning stunned, wondering how I could possibly have had such a dream after finally accepting that I was gay. Could I have made a mistake? Was I really heterosexual? I quickly realized that one heterosexual erotic dream was just that, one heterosexual erotic dream—nothing to get upset about. My feelings for men hadn't changed, and beyond the one dream I had no strong feelings of sexual attraction for women. After talking with friends, I discovered that I wasn't the only gay man who had had a heterosexual erotic dream, and some of my heterosexual friends acknowledged having had homosexual erotic dreams.

> **If you've had a homosexual experience, does that make you gay or lesbian?**
> **If you've had a heterosexual experience, does that make you heterosexual?**

Plenty of heterosexual people have had sexual relations with someone of the same gender, and plenty of gay and lesbian people have had sexual relations with someone of the opposite gender. These experiences have not changed anyone's basic sexual orientation, although they may have broadened a few horizons.

> **Don't heterosexual people who are in same-gender environments engage in homosexual behavior?**
> **Does this make them gay?**

It's not uncommon for heterosexuals in restricted same-gender environments, like prisons, to engage in homosexual behavior. Their sexual orientation remains the same; they are still heterosexual and, given the opportunity, would choose an opposite-gender partner.

> **What should you do if you are heterosexual and fall in love with someone of the opposite gender who is gay or lesbian?**

This question came to me from a woman in Salt Lake City who had fallen in love with her best friend, a gay man. In her letter to me, she explained that she and her friend shared many interests, spent a lot of time together, particularly on weekends, and were also very affectionate toward one another. As far as she knew, her friend had no sexual interest in her and had never been physically involved with a woman. Her hope was that if she disclosed to him her romantic and physical interests, these interests might be reciprocated.

In my return letter, I explained that from what she had told me about her friend, it was unlikely that he would be interested in a romantic and physical relationship with her. But I also told her that she should consider talking to her friend about her feelings. That would give him the opportunity to tell her the extent of his feelings for her, and if his feelings were platonic—as I strongly suspected they were—that would give her the opportunity to lay to rest her yearnings for a more involved relationship. I warned her, however, that there was no guarantee her friend would welcome this conversation and that even if he did, the discussion could be a painful one for her.

In general, if you are heterosexual, falling in love with someone of the opposite gender who is gay is not a great idea, since your feelings are unlikely to be reciprocated. If you can't help it and you find yourself fantasizing about turning your gay or lesbian love interest "straight," you might consider seeing a professional therapist to explore what drives you to pursue someone who is fundamentally unavailable.

> **How many gay and lesbian people are there?**

For many years the commonly accepted figure was that one in ten people were gay or lesbian. This number was based on an interpretation of Alfred Kinsey's landmark studies from the 1940s and 1950s. I was never comfortable reciting that number, because I always thought it was overstated, even accounting for the fact that most gay and lesbian people remain hidden.

Other studies in recent years suggest that the numbers from the Kinsey studies were misinterpreted and that the 10 percent figure is too high. Of all the studies and surveys I've read, the one that seems to make the most sense is a study whose results were published by the University of Chicago Press under the title *The Social Organization of Sexuality*. Conducted in 1993, the study found that the percentage of gay men and women in the population varied widely between the big cities, the suburbs, and rural areas. For example, in the top twelve largest cities, 10.2 percent of the men and 2.1 percent of the women reported having had a sexual partner of their own gender in the last year. In the suburbs of the top twelve cities, 2.7 percent of the men and 1.2 percent of the women reported having had a sexual partner of their own gender in the last year. And for rural areas, the numbers were 1.0 percent for men and 0.6 percent for women.

Overall, the study found that 2.6 percent of men and 1.1 percent of women reported having had a sexual partner of their own gender in the last year. The authors of the study were quick to point out that their numbers were not the last word, in part because many gay and lesbian people were probably reluctant to report certain behaviors or feelings to the interviewers. For this and other reasons—including the fact that the numbers in the study were based on behavior as opposed to feelings of attraction—the actual numbers of gay and lesbian people are likely higher than those reported in the study.

My educated guess is that approximately 5 percent of men and about half that number of women have a same-gender sexual orientation, whether or not they express it by having a relationship of some kind with a person of the same gender. But whatever the actual figures, there are certainly millions of gay and lesbian people in the United States.

> **Have there always been gay and lesbian people?**

There is every reason to believe that there have always been some people who have had feelings of attraction for those of the same gender and some people who have had sexual relationships with those of the same gender. In any case, we know it's been going on for thousands of years, as is evident from historical writings and scenes depicted in ancient art.

> **Why are there so many more gay people today than there were years ago?**

This is a question my grandmother asked me. She told me that she remembers, back in the 1940s, seeing one man on the subway platform in her Brooklyn neighborhood who "held his cigarette a certain way, wore a little makeup, and dressed impeccably." Because of his manner and clothing, she just assumed he was gay, based on the stereotype she had grown up with. "Now you see gay people on television, read about them in the newspaper, and they have parades. Where did they all come from?" she asked.

Gay and lesbian people have always been there, but because most gay men and women look and act just like most nongay people, there was no way for my grandmother to know that there were lots of gay and lesbian people on the subway platform with her. The difference today is that many gay and lesbian people have publicly acknowledged to their friends, family, and colleagues that they're gay.

❯ How do you become a homosexual?

No one becomes a homosexual any more than a man or woman becomes a heterosexual. Feelings of attraction for one gender or the other are something we become aware of as we grow up. Where exactly these feelings come from and why some of us have strong heterosexual feelings while others have strong homosexual feelings has plenty to do with genetics and biology and nothing to do with sin or morality, though many religious fundamentalists would have you believe just the opposite. (See "Are you born gay?" for a more complete answer.)

❯ Is it a choice? Why did you choose to be gay?

I wish there were a simple declarative answer to this question, but to say "No, it's not a choice" doesn't fully answer the question. There are, of course, those who insist that there is a simple declarative answer to this question: "Yes, gay and lesbian people willfully choose to be gay in order to defy fundamental religious and cultural norms." Those people, who generally understand nothing about homosexuality, happen to be wrong.

Gay and lesbian people don't choose their feelings of sexual attraction, just as heterosexual people don't choose theirs. All of us become aware of our feelings of attraction as we grow, whether those feelings are for someone of the same gender, the opposite gender, or both genders. For gay and lesbian people, the only real choice is between suppressing those feelings of same-gender attraction—and pretending to be asexual or heterosexual—and living the full emotional and physical life of a gay man or woman.

Although most people who live a gay or lesbian life do not have a true choice between a same-gender and opposite-gender partner, there are some men and women who have feelings of sexual attraction to both genders and therefore have the option of choosing. So, indeed, for some people there is a choice. One woman I know, who was once married to a man, explained to me that after her divorce, the first person she fell in love with happened to be a woman. "If I had fallen in love with a man first, I would have been in a heterosexual relationship instead," she explained. I hasten to add that this is not the experience of the vast majority of people who live a gay or lesbian life.

❯ Are you born gay?

This debate dates back to the late 1800s, when Magnus Hirschfeld, founder of the first gay rights movement in Germany, stated his belief that homosexuality had biological origins. Now, after a few generations of accepting the psychiatric model for the origins of homosexuality, scientists are once again focusing on the biological/genetic origins of human sexuality. Though no studies have yet concluded unequivocally that sexual orientation is biologically and/or genetically based, the evidence points in that direction.

According to Chandler Burr, the author of *A Separate Creation: The Search for the Biological Origins of Sexual Orientation*, "The evidence, although preliminary, strongly indicates a genetic and biological basis for all sexual orientation. We see this in the work of scientists Michael Bailey and Richard Pillard, who have done studies on twins and gay and lesbian siblings. For example, they found that with identical twins, where one twin is gay, the other twin has an approximately 50 percent chance of being gay. In fraternal twins [separate eggs], if one sibling is gay, there is a 16 percent chance the other sibling will be gay.

And in non-genetically related adopted brothers and sisters, where one sibling is gay or lesbian, there is a 9 percent chance that the other sibling will be homosexual, which is approximately the normal statistical incidence in the general population. These results, which indicate that sexual orientation is governed primarily by genetics, have been confirmed dramatically in other laboratories in the United States."

Burr adds that there are other factors that contribute to sexual orientation, "which may be either biological factors—other than genetics—or 'environmental factors.'" *Environmental factors*, he explains, "is a term that has recently gone through a major metamorphosis in meaning. It once meant large, discrete, identifiable experiences, such as coming in contact with a gay person as a child. We now understand the 'environment' to be quite simply any and all sensory stimulation, which all people receive by virtue of being alive and living in society."

Burr concludes: "Sexual orientation's biological component is effectively determined at birth. And we know conclusively that sexual orientation is neither changeable nor a matter of choice."

I also like what Abigail Van Buren ("Dear Abby"), the internationally respected purveyor of commonsense advice, has to say on this subject: "I've always known that there was nothing wrong with gay and lesbian people, that this is a natural way of life for them. Nobody molested them, nobody talked them into anything. They were simply born that way."

❭ Is homosexuality a mental illness?

No. In response to convincing evidence, as well as concerted lobbying on the part of prominent psychiatrists as well as gay rights activists, the American Psychiatric Association's board of trustees voted in December 1973 to stop classifying homosexuality as a mental illness in the *Diagnostic and Statistical Manual*. The

American Psychological Association followed suit a little more than a year later.

It was in the mid-1950s that the late psychologist Dr. Evelyn Hooker first demonstrated in a landmark study that homosexual men and heterosexual men were no different psychologically. In other words, gay men were on average just as sane as their nongay counterparts.

> **Aren't there psychiatrists and psychologists who say they can "cure" homosexuality?**

Despite the official positions of both the American Psychiatric Association and the American Psychological Association and overwhelming evidence to the contrary, there are still psychiatrists, psychoanalysts, and psychologists who claim that homosexuality is a "curable" mental illness. Others, who don't go so far as to suggest a cure for same-gender attraction, claim that they have achieved "a diminishment of homosexual feelings" among their homosexual patients, enabling them to enter heterosexual marriages and have children. But no matter what anyone claims, you cannot change a person's sexual orientation. In other words, you cannot eliminate a person's feelings of attraction for the same gender any more than you can eliminate a person's feelings of attraction for the opposite gender.

"Dear Abby" once again offers my favorite comment regarding mental health professionals who try to change homosexuals into heterosexuals: "Any therapist who would take a gay person and try to change him or her should be in jail. What the psychiatrist should do is to make the patient more comfortable with what he or she is—to be himself or herself." Amen!

> **What are some of the ways in which mental health experts and doctors have tried to "cure" homosexuals?**

Some mental health professionals who believed homosexual people were mentally ill or physically sick tried to "cure" gay men and lesbians by using a variety of techniques, including electroshock therapy, brain surgery, hormone injections, and even castration. Other methods included aversion therapy, in which, for example, male homosexuals were shown erotic pictures of men at the same time that an electric shock was applied to their genitals or they were induced to vomit.

While "curing" homosexuality is no longer the goal of mainstream mental health professionals, there are organizations that maintain programs to help gay people "change" their orientation, and some of these groups employ a number of the now discredited methods.

❯ Can you be seduced into being gay?

Whenever I'm asked this question I can't help but picture a heavyset, middle-aged, balding man dressed in a trench coat hiding in the bushes trying to lure young boys with candy. Despite this and other false stereotypes of how boys and girls are allegedly "lured" into a homosexual life, it is simply not true that a person can be seduced into being gay. A heterosexual person can't be seduced into being a gay man or lesbian any more than you can seduce a gay man or lesbian into being a heterosexual.

❯ Do gay men and lesbians recruit people to become gay?

No, gay men and lesbians do not recruit people to become gay. At best, gay and lesbian people can serve as positive role models for those who are struggling with their gay and lesbian identities. They can show by example that you can be a gay or lesbian person and lead a full and happy life—at least as happy as anyone else's. But despite what some people may claim, gay and lesbian people do not recruit heterosexual children or adults.

❯ Are gay and lesbian people more likely to molest children?

Absolutely not. The most likely person to molest children is a heterosexual male. His most likely victim is a female child. For example, a study conducted by Children's Hospital in Denver found that between July 1, 1991, and June 30, 1992, only 1 of 387 cases of suspected child molestation involved a gay perpetrator. Overwhelmingly, the study found that boys and girls alike said they were abused by heterosexual male family members, including fathers, stepfathers, grandfathers, and uncles.

According to Frank Bruni, a journalist who has written extensively about child molestation, "Men who molest prepubescent boys are most often—by a wide margin—heterosexual in any adult sexual involvements they may have." Bruni is the coauthor, with Ellinor Burkett, of *A Gospel of Shame: Children, Sexual Abuse, and the Catholic Church.*

> **Do parents raise a child to be homosexual?**
> **Aren't gay people the result of domineering mothers and passive fathers?**

You can't "raise" a child to be gay. This misconception, unfortunately, is supported by Sigmund Freud's flawed and long since outdated theory that a homosexual male child is the result of a strong mother and a passive, indifferent, or hostile father. Among the many flaws in Freud's theory is its failure to explain the countless examples of heterosexual sons raised by strong mothers and passive fathers and of gay sons raised by strong fathers and passive mothers. Freud also fails to explain what combination of parental personality traits leads to a lesbian daughter.

My mother and father were both strong parents, so based on Freud's theory of homosexuality, I should probably be bisexual. But I'm not, and both my sister and brother are heterosexual. Go figure.

> **Is a gay person someone who was sexually abused?**

There is no evidence to suggest that sexual abuse has an impact on whether a child has a same-gender or opposite-gender orientation.

> **Do women become lesbians because they've had bad experiences with men?**

> **Do men become gay because they've had bad experiences with women?**

If all the women who have had bad experiences with men became lesbians, there wouldn't be any heterosexual women. The fact is, bad experiences with men do not "make" heterosexual women lesbians. And bad experiences with women do not "make" heterosexual men gay. The same goes for gay and lesbian people. A bad experience with someone of the same gender does not "make" them heterosexual.

> **Are people gay because they haven't met the right man or woman?**

No. How many heterosexual men and women have embarked on the challenge of "turning" a gay man or lesbian "straight," thinking that they are the "right man" or "right woman" to do the job? Before you try—and I suggest that you don't—you should know that a heterosexual woman cannot make a gay man heterosexual any more than a lesbian can make a heterosexual woman a lesbian. And a heterosexual man cannot turn a lesbian into a heterosexual any more than a gay man can make a heterosexual man a homosexual.

> **Why would you want to be a lesbian when you're already oppressed as a woman?**

> **Why with the threat of AIDS would you want to be a gay man?**

Whether or not a gay woman or man *wants* to have feelings of attraction for the same gender, that's how she or he feels. And no matter how difficult the circumstances—whether it's sexism, the threat of AIDS, antigay violence, job discrimination, or rejection by family—these feelings of same-gender attraction will not change.

❯ Can't gay people be heterosexuals if they want to be?

No, but plenty try to lead a heterosexual life. The condemnation of homosexuality in our society is so great that many, if not most, gay and lesbian people pretend to be heterosexual, at least for part of their lives. Many lead heterosexual lives, complete with opposite-gender spouses and a house full of kids. Some pretend for a lifetime, never acting on their attractions, perhaps never sharing with anyone their true feelings, taking their secret to the grave. Others find ways to accommodate their same-gender feelings through clandestine relationships and affairs. Still others manage to stay married for years but ultimately divorce and seek same-gender relationships.

❯ Are gay people normal?

If normal means "in the majority," then gay and lesbian people are not normal. But if we accept this point, then we also have to say that left-handed people are not normal, yet today we accept this physical variation as completely normal. Like left-handedness, being gay doesn't diminish anyone's humanity—his or her normal wish to love, be loved, and contribute to society.

❯ Isn't homosexuality unnatural?

Gay and lesbian people who are comfortable with their sexuality will tell you that their experience of being with someone of the same gender feels perfectly natural, whereas being with someone of the opposite gender feels unnatural. But often the underlying assumption of those who argue that homosexuality is unnatural is that penile-vaginal intercourse is the only natural way to be sexually active. If we accept this assumption, then heterosexuals who engage in sexual activity other than penile-vaginal intercourse are unnatural as well.

There are also those who argue that the sexual act is unnatural unless it involves the possibility of procreation. But that argument fails to recognize the many heterosexuals who practice birth control or who, for whatever reason, are unable to procreate.

> ❯ **Are humans the only animals that engage in homosexual behavior?**

Scientists have observed consistent homosexual behavior in the animal kingdom in many different species, ranging from mountain rams and seagulls to gorillas. No one has yet suggested that this is the result of a passive father and a domineering mother.

> ❯ **Is homosexuality nature's way of controlling the population?**

If that were nature's purpose, she hasn't succeeded, primarily because many, if not most, gay and lesbian people—even to this day—hide their sexual feelings, enter heterosexual marriages, and have children. Besides which, a growing number of gay and lesbian individuals and couples who live openly are choosing to have children.

> ❯ **How can you tell who is a lesbian?**
> ❯ **How can you tell who is a gay man?**
> ❯ **Why are gay men effeminate and lesbians masculine?**

For the most part, you can't tell who is gay or lesbian from appearances, unless the man or woman in question is wearing a button, a symbol, or a style of clothing that explicitly identifies him or her as gay or lesbian.

At one time the common assumption was that gay and lesbian people were all easily identifiable by well-established stereotypical mannerisms, affectations, dress, and so on. All lesbians were thought to be masculine, and all gay men were thought to be effeminate. In fact, many effeminate men—but not all—are gay, and many masculine women—but not all—are lesbians. By and large, gay and lesbian people, like all people, come in all shapes, sizes, colors, and ages, as well as degrees of masculinity and femininity.

> ❯ *Why do gay men lisp? Is it a chosen affectation?*

Some gay men lisp, as do some heterosexual men. A lisp is a type of speech defect—not a chosen affectation—in which s is pronounced like th. For some reason it has been associated with the gay male stereotype.

Richard, who was tortured in grade school by other students because of his lisp, worked with a speech therapist for years to get rid of it. According to him, "It's ridiculous to suggest that anyone would intentionally choose to do something that would be the source of so much misery. The other kids called me a faggot, and I'm not even gay."

Do more gay men than nongay men lisp? That's one of those mysterious human questions that remains to be answered.

> ❯ *Among gay men, is it more valued to be masculine or to be feminine?*

Within American culture, masculinity in men is, in general, highly valued. Gay men are raised in the same culture as everyone else, so it should come as no surprise that masculinity is highly valued by many, if not most, gay men.

> ❯ *Among lesbians, is it more valued to be feminine or masculine?*

The young woman who suggested I include this question said that both masculinity and femininity are valued among lesbians. Masculinity—traits that are typically associated with masculine behavior, such as aggressiveness and self-confidence—is valued by women in general, she said. And femininity—physically feminine traits—is valued by many lesbians because it allows them to fit comfortably into society.

But another woman I spoke with thought that this question oversimplified the issues. She said: "What is feminine? What is masculine? My aim is to redefine those things. If we had a broader definition of what a man was and what masculinity was we would not be disturbed by people who are different from one narrow little stereotype." She added, "I'm not someone who sits around and worries about defining myself as feminine or masculine. Whoever I am is what a woman is, and it doesn't have to fit into categories of femininity and masculinity. Now, everybody is different. We are an enormously large population. You name it, we've got it. There are old bull dykes who wear pants and a vest and smoke cigars. And there are ballerinas, stewardesses, and secretaries who are lesbian as well. There is a whole spectrum of people in all communities, and the problem is that instead of recognizing our diversity, we assume we are the standard, and then we point at other people and try to narrow them and stereotype them. That's inappropriate."

> ### Why don't lesbians wear makeup? Why don't they shave?

Some gay women wear makeup, some don't, and for all kinds of reasons. Jane doesn't wear makeup. "It runs on my face," she said. "I can't be bothered." Katharine said she wears makeup because she looks "so much better." Another woman added that among some women "there is certainly the attitude that painting oneself is something you do to seduce men by some kind of game playing, so for lesbians that's irrelevant." These same points also apply to the shaving question. I should also add that there are plenty of heterosexual women who don't wear makeup and/or don't shave.

> ### Why do lesbians "have a thing" for cats?

Some lesbians love cats. Some lesbians hate cats. No scientific survey has ever been conducted to establish whether lesbians own more cats per capita than any other group of people. This sounds like an ideal topic of market research for the people who sell cat food and related products.

> ### Why do gay men have better taste and fashion sense than heterosexual men?

Some gay men do indeed have better taste and fashion sense than many nongay men. But from what I've seen there are also gay men who have terrible taste and awful fashion sense and some nongay men who have great taste and superb fashion sense.

> ### Is there a gay and lesbian culture?

I thought I'd offer an explanation of gay culture given to me by the late Chuck Rowland, one of the original founders of the Mattachine Society, a gay organization started in Los Angeles in 1950. Rowland was one of the first people to argue that there was a gay and lesbian culture. When I interviewed him in 1989, he told me that he had an especially hard time in the 1950s explaining to other gay people what he meant by *gay culture*. "People would say, 'Gay culture? What do you mean? Do you actually think we're more cultured than anybody else?' I would explain that I was using *culture* in the sociological sense—as a body of language, feelings, thinking, experiences that we share in common. As we speak of a Mexican culture. As we speak of an American Indian culture.

"We had to say that gay culture was an emergent culture. For example, as gay people, we used certain language, certain words. The word *gay* itself is a marvelous example of what I mean by gay culture. You'll get a lot of argument about this. But I know that *gay* was being used back in the thirties, and we didn't mean 'merry' or 'festive.' We meant 'homosexual.' This does not constitute a language in the sense that English is a language and French is a language, but it's more comparable to Yiddish culture. A lot of people, Jews and non-Jews, use Yiddish words like *schlepp, meshuga,* a dozen others. This separates them culturally from my mother, for example, who would never have heard of such words. A lot of people still don't agree with the gay culture issue. But you see the term *gay culture* all the time now."

In the decades since Chuck Rowland first made his case for the existence of gay culture, a very significant body of work that we would normally associate with the cultural life of a community has been created primarily for gay and lesbian people by gay and lesbian writers, artists, photographers, playwrights, choreographers, filmmakers, and so forth.

> ### *Why do some gay people want to be called "queer"?*

Plenty of gay and lesbian people are puzzled by this one as well. Beginning in the early 1990s, some gay and lesbian people, particularly college students and the more politically radical, chose to use the word *queer* to identify themselves because they felt it was more inclusive than *gay* and *lesbian.* They felt that by "reclaiming" a word that had been used by those who hate gay people, they stripped it of its original hurtful intent and transformed it into something positive.

According to one woman I interviewed who was in her mid-twenties at the time, "While some people find this word offensive, many of us find it liberating because it is a word that embraces us all. We use it as a word of pride, of inclusion, and of community. The word reflects the painful reality that regardless of how we identify ourselves, we are all outside the heterosexual majority, and we all suffer prejudice, discrimination, hatred, and ignorance from the majority population."

After enjoying some popularity for several years, the word queer is now used mostly in an academic context, as in "Queer Studies." (See chapter 16, "Education.") It also continues in its traditional role as an epithet.

> **Why do some gay and lesbian people call themselves "fags" and "dykes"?**

Like other minority groups, some gay and lesbian people playfully use words that are used by the larger population to put them down. Some say it's a way of taking the sting out of these words.

Warning: In general, you can use these words playfully only if you yourself are gay or lesbian. And bear in mind that plenty of gay and lesbian people do not like the words fag and dyke no matter the sexual orientation of the person using them. Of course, there are exceptions. A gay male friend of mine who lives in Chelsea, a New York City neighborhood with a very large population of gay men, has heterosexual female friends, who also live in the neighborhood, who use the word fag while in his company. He knows they're simply being playful and is not at all bothered by it.

> **What does breeders mean?**

A man I know was standing at the counter of an ice cream shop on Castro Street, the commercial heart of San Francisco's predominantly gay and lesbian neighborhood. While he was ordering ice cream for himself and his adopted daughter, a gay man standing beside him at the counter turned to him and said with a sneer, "Breeder." This is a term, not exactly affectionate, that some gay people use to describe heterosexuals—

that is, heterosexuals who have children, or "breeders." Unfortunately, the man who called my acquaintance a breeder mistakenly assumed that he was heterosexual. In fact, he's a gay man in a long-term relationship raising a daughter. This just goes to show that gay people can also make stereotyped assumptions and say hateful things.

> *What do I do if a gay person makes a pass at me?*

If you're not interested, you say, "No thank you." If you are interested, you can make your interest known in a variety of ways. (See chapter 5, "Dating.")

> *What is the "gay lifestyle"?*

There is no such thing as a "gay lifestyle," just as there is no such thing as a "heterosexual lifestyle." Homosexuality, like heterosexuality, is a sexual orientation, not a lifestyle. Gay and lesbian people, like nongay people, live a variety of lifestyles, which may be very similar to yours or quite different.

Several years ago, just after I moved back to New York following the end of a long-term relationship, a woman friend told me that she was worried I'd go out and lead a wild "gay lifestyle." Based on her misconceptions about the lives gay men lead, my friend feared that I would go out to a gay club, dance all night, drink too much, take drugs, probably strip off my shirt when things got too hot, and maybe even have unsafe sex in the balcony overlooking the dance floor. Of course, some gay men live a wild, urban, single lifestyle—as do some heterosexual men—but given what my friend knew about me and the life I had led in the past, this was hardly a likely scenario for me.

> *Don't gay people make more money?*

Although accurate statistics are hard to come by, gay people, on average, are as diverse in the amount of money they earn as are nongay people. However, those gay and lesbian people who do not have children to support, like those heterosexual people who do not have children to support, have higher disposable incomes.

When it comes to gay and lesbian couples, there is a notable difference in combined income in comparison to heterosexual couples, whether or not there are children to support. Gay male couples are likely to have higher combined incomes than heterosexual couples because two men are likely to earn more money than a man and a woman; on average, women are paid less than men. By contrast, lesbian couples, on average, have lower combined incomes than heterosexual couples because two women are likely to earn less money than a man and a woman.

> **Do gay men hate women?**
> **Do lesbians hate men?**

In general, no. But some gay men do hate women, just as some heterosexual men hate women. And some gay men hate men, despite the fact they have feelings of attraction for men. And some lesbians hate men, just as some heterosexual women hate men. And some lesbians hate women, despite the fact they have feelings of attraction for women. The bottom line is, everyone is capable of hating, no matter what his or her sexual orientation or gender.

> **Do gay men and lesbians hate nongay people?**

Some gay and lesbian people have hostile feelings toward heterosexual people. This should come as no surprise, given some of the terrible things gay and lesbian people have experienced at the hands of heterosexual people. (See chapter 12, "Discrimination and Antigay Violence.") But, as a rule, gay men and women don't hate nongay people.

2

—

?

SELF-DISCOVERY: GROWING UP

> ❯ When do you first become aware of your homosexual feelings?
>
> ❯ Is there any difference between men and women with regard to when they become aware of their homosexual feelings?

People who have feelings of attraction for the same gender most often become aware of these feelings at the same time all people become aware of their feelings of attraction, whether that's from earliest conscious memory or during preadolescence or adolescence, or later. But there are differences. For heterosexual people these feelings of attraction are reinforced—by family, society, culture, religion—from the earliest age. For example, how many times have you heard loving relatives ask a young child if he has a girlfriend or she has a boyfriend? Even if it's asked in the most playful way, this question reinforces the idea that boys have girlfriends and girls have boyfriends.

For a gay or lesbian child growing up, the experience is very different. Even before they're fully aware of their feelings of attraction or the implications of those feelings, gay and lesbian kids know that what they're feeling isn't how things are supposed to be. That was Deborah's experience: "Growing up was quite traumatic for me because I really thought that I was a little boy trapped inside a little girl's body. I was supposed to be sweet and docile, but I was a jock. I wanted to grab the world by the balls! It just didn't make any sense to me. And I had sexual feelings very, very early, but boys were not an interest. When the other little girls were starting to get crushes on boys and were talking about weddings, I always knew I wanted to marry a girl—always, always, always. When I was seven, I remember telling my parents that I was not going to marry a man and all the reasons why. By the time I was ten, I explained to them that I was in love with this little girl. My dad told me that it was just a phase, that I was going to outgrow it.

"I didn't know there was such a thing as lesbianism, women with women, so I just assumed that I would have to be a male if I wanted to be with women. It was very confusing. It was when I read the play *The Children's Hour* in seventh grade that I learned about women with women. I was doing a scene with this woman I had a serious crush on, and she got to the part where she explained how she really felt for her female coworker. It hit me like a ton of bricks: 'That's what this is!'"

Beyond the confusion of not understanding why you're different from other kids, and the confusion of having a parent tell you that you'll "outgrow it," for example, gay and lesbian kids often get daily negative reinforcement of what they're feeling, whether that's religious condemnation of homosexuality, kids using the words *fag* and *dyke* and *lezzie* at school, or jokes about gay people in the movies. Because of this negative reinforcement, most gay and lesbian people hide their sexual orientation, pretend to be heterosexual, and wait at least until after high school to deal with their sexual orientation and act on their feelings. Some gay and lesbian people may repress their feelings of sexual attraction for years and may lead heterosexual lives that include marriage, children, and grandchildren without ever telling another soul about their homosexuality.

Some gay people—and generally I hear this from women, rarely from men—don't become fully aware of their feelings of attraction until they reach their thirties, forties, or later. That was Mary Elizabeth's experience: "When I was still in my teens, Mother used to tell me not to wear my hair short or wear tailored clothing. I never understood what she was talking about. It took me until I was nearly forty-five, married, with two grown kids to figure out what she was getting at. Mother was afraid that if I looked and dressed like a lesbian, I'd become one. Mother knew what was up long before I did! I sure as hell wish she'd said something to me before she died, because it took me forever to realize what she knew all along. I know some people won't believe this, but I really didn't know I had these feelings until I fell in love with Eileen. And she was married, too!"

> **Do people who are gay or lesbian feel bad about it?**
> **Do they always feel this way?**
> **Why are gay and lesbian people so angry?**

Feel bad? When I was a teenager, I thought my life was over. How could I be something that was considered so disgusting, so loathsome, so awful? How could I be what people called a homo, a queer, a sissy, a child molester, a fag? (At the time I grew up, there were virtually no positive gay images or role models.) What I didn't know until later was that feeling bad about my attraction to men was a perfectly normal reaction to what I had learned from the world around me about homosexuals and the life I could expect to lead.

Just as I did by my early twenties, plenty of gay and lesbian people go on to accept their sexual orientation. But many people find that feelings of self-hate, fear, and guilt are transformed into feelings of rage and anger. People feel angry about being lied to by religious leaders, judged by their parents, misled by psychiatrists, and condemned by society in general. They're angry at their lost adolescence, or in the case of people who don't come to accept their sexuality until later in life, they're angry about having "wasted" their lives living a lie. In time, for most gay and lesbian people, this anger recedes—although it doesn't necessarily go away.

Gay and lesbian people can also find themselves angered at any time in life when confronted by discrimination, antigay propaganda, and antigay violence. For example, in 1998, the murder of Matthew Shepard, a gay college student in Wyoming, who was pistol-whipped, burned, and left to die tied to a fence in subfreezing temperatures, infuriated gay and lesbian people—as well as many heterosexuals— across the country. Shepard was chosen as a target because he was gay.

> **Do all gay men and women feel bad about being gay as they become aware of their orientation?**

No. Not every gay or lesbian person goes through the experience of feeling bad about himself or herself. This has been especially true in recent years as gay and lesbian people have been more visible in society, providing positive role models for gay kids. Dan, who grew up in suburban Detroit, knew exactly what he was from the second grade on and also knew that there was nothing wrong: "I don't know how I knew I was okay and the world was wrong, but I just knew it. In elementary school I liked other boys, and that felt right to me, so from then on I never paid attention to the name-calling. And besides that, my uncle is gay and everyone loves him, so being gay was never a big deal in my family. Sure, my parents weren't thrilled when I told them, but that was mostly because they worried about discrimination and AIDS."

> **How do gay people accept that they are gay or lesbian?**

Many, if not most, gay and lesbian people have difficulty in accepting their orientation because accepting these feelings of same-gender attraction means unlearning what are likely to be deeply held negative beliefs about homosexuals and homosexuality.

People learn to accept themselves through a variety of means. They may do their own personal research, reading everything they can find on the subject of homosexuality, or they may find role models in their families or their communities. They may also join support groups for gay and lesbian people or enter therapy.

Not everyone who is gay or lesbian accepts it. Some people struggle to repress what they're feeling, denying even to themselves what they know in their hearts and minds. Some people search for a "cure" through therapy, religion, or an organization that promises to show them "the way out of the homosexual lifestyle." There is, of course, no cure for homosexuality, because you can no more cure a person's feelings of same-gender attraction than you can cure a person's feelings of opposite-gender attraction.

> **Do gay people like being gay or lesbian?**

This question reminds me of a related question that I've often been asked: If you could take a pill and become a heterosexual, would you? This question presumes that life would be better as a heterosexual. When I was seventeen, I would have said yes in a second. I didn't like being gay. I wanted to be "normal." I wanted to be like everyone else. I wanted to find a relationship, get married, hold hands on the street, and be able to proclaim my love for another person in public. I didn't want to be different. But by the time I was in my early twenties, I wasn't so sure I wanted to take such a pill, because my life as a gay man wasn't so bad, and I was getting used to it. Also, from what I saw, I knew there was no guarantee that life would be any better as a heterosexual person, and it could also be worse. By my mid-twenties I realized this was a ridiculous question, because there was no such pill, and by then I had already decided that there were far more difficult things in life than being gay, and I should make the most of who I was, even if that was something society didn't like. Now I wouldn't want to be any different, because I like who I am, and part of that is being gay. I've also been blessed with a happy relationship, a supportive family, and a good life. So why would I want to be any different?

I don't pretend to speak for everyone, but when Ann Landers asked her readers to write in and tell her if they were glad to be gay, she got tens of thousands of letters in response, most of them (thirty to one) from gay and lesbian people who were glad to be who they were. (Of course, there are also many gay and lesbian people who are not happy about who they are, but I imagine they were less likely to make the effort to respond to the Ann Landers column.)

I put this question to several different gay and lesbian people and they offered several different responses. Among those who like being gay, some people said they can't imagine being any different. Others feel that they're more sensitive and more insightful people because of their experience of growing up in a world where they were outsiders. Others feel lucky to have been given the opportunity to lead something other than a traditional life in which you progress from single life to marriage to children without thinking about whether that is something you really want to do. The experience of growing up gay, many told me, led them to ask questions about life's assumptions—that they would, for example, get married and have children—that most heterosexual people never examine.

Those who had negative feelings about being gay also offered a variety of reasons for their feelings. Some said they would have better luck finding a spouse if they were heterosexual, or that being gay has held them back in their careers, or that being gay has made it difficult to have children.

> *What's it like to be a gay or lesbian teenager?*
> *What's it like for gay and lesbian kids in high school?*

I have only a handful of vivid memories of my high school years, a time when I was just beginning to come to terms with being gay. One of those memories is from a Sunday afternoon party in the spring of 1976, during my senior year at Hillcrest High School in New York City. About twenty of us were scattered around the living room of a friend's apartment. Across from where I was standing, my friend Ruth was sitting on a big easy chair, with her boyfriend on one arm of the chair and our friend Dave on the other. I was pretty sure by then that Dave was gay; we'd started dropping hints to each other a few weeks before. (We even admitted to each other that we might be bisexual.) Everyone was listening to Ruth, who somehow worked her way onto the subject of gay people and declared, "I guess it's okay with me, but I wouldn't want one of them near me." Instantly, Dave and I locked eyes. Ruth had no idea that the man sitting next to her was gay (Dave told me he was gay after we graduated) and that the friend who picked her up every day for three years to go to school—me!—was also gay.

"What would she think?" I wondered. "Would she still want to be my friend?"

The two emotions that most dominated my life at that time were fear and a sense of isolation. I was fearful of what my friends and family would think of me if they knew the truth, and I felt enormous isolation because there was no one I could talk to. I'd hoped that this had changed for teenagers growing up today. But while I know that for some gay teens things are better—particularly for those lucky adolescents who go to high schools where there are counselors and organizations for them to turn to for help—many of the letters I receive from kids around the country today are heartbreaking. Most of the teens I hear from are scared and isolated, living in fear of their own friends and family, with no one to talk to about what they're going through. More than a few have written to tell me, "You're the only person who knows." Most of the kids I hear from do everything they can to pass as nongay and keep their sexual orientation a secret from everyone they know. And from my research, I know that the experience of these teenagers is more typical than not.

Elliott, who is finishing high school early to get away from his tormentors at his suburban Dallas high school, is just one example. He told me: "Since the very first day, some of the kids have called me 'sissy' and 'fag' in the halls. They try to trip me all the time, and someone once wrote 'AIDS victim' on my locker. It's been absolute hell." Elliott hasn't had much better luck with his mother. He moved out of her house at the start of his senior year and now lives with a friend's family several blocks away: "My mom didn't want me meeting other gay people, so I'd have to sneak out. Of course, she caught me a few times, and it got real ugly. I had to get away."

There are, thankfully, exceptions. Tammy, who is now in college, found a group of supportive friends—gay and nongay—on her high school volleyball team. "I always knew I was lucky," she said, "to have a group of friends when I was that young I didn't have to keep secrets from. It really helped me accept being gay. There were a couple of other lesbians on the team, and we were all out to each other and the rest of the team. I don't know, maybe it was just the right time or it was the right group of people, or maybe it's finally sinking in that there's nothing wrong with us."

> ### Are there organizations specifically for gay and lesbian teenagers?

The most common organizations for gay, lesbian, bisexual, and transgender teenagers are the more than five hundred gay/straight alliances (GSAs) at high schools across the country. The first GSA was founded in 1991, and since then, through the coordinating efforts of the Student Pride Program of the Gay, Lesbian & Straight Education Network (GLSEN), the idea has spread like wildfire. (See chapter 16, "Education," for more on GLSEN). The purpose of the GSAs is to provide a supportive and safe forum for open discussion between gay and nongay students about the issues gay students are facing in school, with their families, and with their communities. The groups are open to all students, and no student has to identify his or her own sexual orientation. For information about finding a local GSA or starting one at your high school, contact GLSEN (see "Resources").

In addition to the GSAs, there are more than ninety different organizations across the country that provide a range of services for gay, lesbian, bisexual, and transgender youth, from peer counseling to education. These organizations are members of the National Youth Advocacy Coalition (NYAC), which according to its official statement is the only national organization that focuses "solely on improving the lives of gay, lesbian, bisexual, and transgender youth through advocacy, education and information. NYAC advocates for and with gay, lesbian, bisexual, and transgender youth through the collaboration of a broad spectrum of community-based and national organizations. Through this partnership, NYAC seeks to end discrimination against gay, lesbian, bisexual, and transgender youth and to ensure their physical and emotional well-being. NYAC's Bridges Project provides information resources, technical assistance, and referrals to gay, lesbian, bisexual, and transgender youth and their allies."

To find a local youth organization and other youth resources—including crisis hot lines, publications, and pen pal groups—contact NYAC (see "Resources" at the end of the book).

> ### What do heterosexual teenagers think of their gay and lesbian peers?

Nongay teenagers have a whole range of feelings toward their gay and lesbian peers, from easy acceptance to thoughts and acts of physical violence. Two reports—a 1997 survey of nearly four thousand Massachusetts high school students and a 1998 study of about five hundred community college students in the San Francisco area—paint a disturbing picture. As reported in the New York Times, in the Massachusetts study, 22 percent of the gay and lesbian respondents said they had skipped school in the past month because they felt unsafe at their high school and 31 percent said they had been threatened or injured at school in the past year. (These percentages were about five times greater than the percentages for the heterosexual respondents.)

In the San Francisco study, 32 percent of the male respondents said they had verbally threatened homosexuals and 18 percent said they had physically threatened or assaulted them. Add to these disturbing reports a 1997 study conducted in Des Moines, Iowa, by a student group called Concerned Students. The group recorded hallway and classroom conversations at five high schools on ten "homophobia recording days." They estimated that the average Des Moines high school student heard about twenty-five antigay remarks every day.

These studies give insight into what some heterosexual teens think of their homosexual peers. But it certainly isn't the whole picture. For example, one woman I spoke with, who travels to New York City high school classrooms to educate students about gay and lesbian people, offered another perspective. She told me: "Many of these heterosexual teenagers are furious at their gay or lesbian peers for hiding. They think they're liars and cheats and deceivers and manipulators. But the fact is, these gay and lesbian kids are afraid—mostly of being rejected. So when you explain to teenagers what's really going on—that these gay and lesbian kids are not being criminals or betrayers—and explain how much pain and terror they're experiencing, then they say, 'Oh, I get it. I didn't want to be mean to that person for that.' I also tell these kids, 'It's up to you to make the first move. Do not expect your gay and lesbian friends to come to you and tell you they're gay if you have not given them a signal that it's okay to talk to you.'"

> *What do students learn about homosexuality in elementary school and high school?*
> *Are there high schools especially for gay and lesbian teens?*

See chapter 16, "Education."

> *Do gay teens take same-gender dates to the high school prom? Why, or why not?*

Most gay and lesbian teenagers don't take same-gender dates to their high school proms, and for many reasons: They haven't yet come to terms with their sexual orientation or aren't yet fully aware of these feelings, so they wouldn't think of taking a same-gender date to the prom. They don't want the other students to know that they're gay or lesbian. They're fearful of how other students will react. They don't want their parents to find out that they're gay or lesbian. They don't want to be the focus of attention or can't find a date willing to be the focus of attention, which a same-gender couple most certainly will be. Or, like plenty of heterosexual kids, they simply can't find a date.

The earliest stories I came across about high school students taking same-gender dates to proms involved two young men at a high school in Medford, Massachusetts, in 1975, and two young women at Girls High in Philadelphia in 1976. Through the years, some students who have brought same-gender dates have been welcomed and others have had to fight school administrations determined to prevent a student from bringing a same-gender date to a school prom.

Teenagers who take same-gender dates to their high school proms usually do it for the same reason heterosexual teenagers do: because they want to go with the date of their choice. As Aaron Fricke wrote in 1980 in his landmark book *Reflections of a Rock Lobster*, about his experience of having to sue his high school in Cumberland, Rhode Island, in order to bring his male date: "The simple, obvious thing would have been to go to the senior prom with a girl. But that would have been a lie—a lie to myself, to the girl, and to all the other students. What I *wanted* to do was to take a male date."

But beyond the desire to be true to himself, Fricke wanted to make a statement about who he was and his rights as a gay person. He wrote: "I concluded that taking a guy to the prom would be a strong positive statement about the existence of gay people. Any opposition to my case (and I anticipated a good bit) would show the negative side of society—not homosexuality."

Besides individual acts of courage, some organizations have sponsored gay proms for young people. For example, beginning in 1995, the Hayward, California, Lambda Youth Group, with the assistance of the United Way, Horizon Services, and private donations, sponsored the Gay Prom '95, which was designed to attract gay and lesbian people sixteen to twenty-one years of age from the San Francisco Bay Area. The drug- and alcohol-free event drew two hundred teenagers and young adults. The following year, eight hundred prom-goers attended.

> **If you're a teenager and think you're gay or lesbian, what should you do?**

If you think you're gay, lesbian, bisexual, whatever, and you haven't got anyone to talk to about your feelings, find someone you can trust—and talk. You'll feel better if you share what you're thinking with someone else. If there isn't anyone in your life you can trust—a best friend, a sibling, a school counselor—you have other options. In many cities, in addition to high school gay/straight alliances (see "Resources," at the end of the book for GSA contact information), there are discussion groups just for gay, lesbian, and bisexual young people and scores of local organizations that provide a range of services for gay, lesbian, bisexual, and transgender youth. You can find these groups by looking in the phone book, calling a local gay help line, searching the Internet, or contacting the National Youth Advocacy Coalition (see "Resources"). You can also contact Parents, Families and Friends of Lesbians and Gays (PFLAG). At PFLAG you'll find an accepting mom or dad who has lots of experience with these issues and will be more than happy to talk to you. Ask for the chapter nearest to where you live (see "Resources").

3

?

COMING OUT: GOING PUBLIC

> *What does "coming out of the closet" mean?*

To understand how a gay or lesbian person "comes out of the closet," you first need to know what "the closet" is. The closet is simply a metaphor used to describe the place where gay and lesbian people keep their sexual orientation hidden—whether that place is between their ears, within a tightly knit group of friends, or within the larger gay and lesbian community. The truth is kept "in the closet, behind the closet door."

At its most basic, "coming out of the closet" means being honest with those around you—friends, family, colleagues, and so forth—about your sexual orientation, about who you are. For example, that might mean talking about your same-gender spouse if a new colleague asks you if you're married. But coming out of the closet means different things to different people. When you ask three different gay and lesbian people to talk about their coming-out experiences, you're likely to get three entirely different stories. One person will talk about coming out sexually—his or her first sexual experience. Another will talk about coming out to herself—when she first accepted the fact that she was a lesbian. Still another will talk about coming out to his family—when he first told his family that he was gay.

› *What's it like living in the closet?*

"It's exhausting and frightening," said Beverly, who spent more than a dozen years in the military hiding the fact that she was a lesbian. "I never knew when the ax would fall, when someone would turn me in. At any moment I knew my career could be over. So I watched everything I said, everything I did, to make sure no one would guess the truth. I tell you, it was the hardest thing I ever did in my life. I thought I was going to lose my mind."

Even if your job doesn't depend on keeping your sexual orientation hidden, staying in the closet can be hard work. You've got to live two different lives—your real life, and a life that's suitable for public consumption. You have to monitor what you say and be careful of what you do, and you have to make certain your two lives never intersect. When you attend office functions, you've got to bring a date of the opposite gender, even if you've been living with your same-gender partner for twenty years. When your kids visit you and your same-gender spouse for the weekend, you have to pretend that you're roommates and make certain you've left no incriminating evidence—a book or magazine, for example—anywhere in the house. (Kids are curious, and if there's something to be found, they'll find it.) Above all, you've got to be an expert storyteller. You've got to be able to tell a convincing lie with a straight face.

When I was a teenager, I was terribly frightened that people would find out I was gay. I worked hard to keep my secret, and I made up all kinds of stories to cover my tracks. Once when I was home on vacation during my first year in college, I went out with some gay friends on a Friday night. I told my mother some story about where I was going and with whom. And I told my girlfriend from high school, who was also home from college, something about having gone to a party. I didn't mean to tell two different stories, but I couldn't remember what I'd told my mother. So there we were the next evening, the three of us, in the living room at my mother's house, and Eileen asked me how my Friday night party had been. Well, I couldn't remember what story I'd told my mother, but it was clear from the expression on her face that I hadn't told her I was at a party. Eileen saw the expression on my mother's face and the look of horror on my face, and there was a split second when everyone realized I'd been caught in a lie. It was in that moment that I realized I didn't have the talent—or the memory—required to keep my life a secret. I was a failure at staying in the closet. Fortunately, I have a family that accepts me as I am and a career that doesn't require me to hide.

Many people are experts at keeping their homosexuality carefully hidden and don't find it especially difficult. Tom is in his early fifties, in a relationship with a man for more than two decades, and deep in the closet to everyone but his close circle of gay male friends. As far as his colleagues know, he's a confirmed bachelor who has no life beyond his career. Tom explains: "I learned a long time ago how to keep my two worlds—my personal life and my professional life—entirely separate. I never socialize with people from work and never discuss anything about my personal life with my colleagues. My partner and I have separate phones at home, both of which are unlisted, so even if someone suspected I had a male spouse, they could never trace us through the phone company.

"I would never have gotten as far as I have in my career if it were known that I'm gay, and I'm not about to risk all I have just so I can bring my partner to company parties. It's not worth it. Years ago, when I was growing up, there was no choice. No one ever talked about coming out of the closet, because it would have been such an outrageous thing to do. Only crazy people didn't hide. You *had* to keep it hidden. Now there's a choice, but I'm happy and very comfortable with the way I live my life."

> ### Why do people stay in the closet?

Gay and lesbian people stay in the closet for three primary reasons: necessity, fear, and because they simply prefer or are accustomed to discussing that part of their lives with only a select group of people.

Those who stay in the closet because of necessity may do so because they know or suspect they'll lose their jobs or, for example, because they think their parents will stop paying their college tuition or throw them out of the house if they find out.

Those who hide their sexual orientation out of fear may fear being rejected by their families, losing or compromising their careers, losing custody of their children, being thrown out of the house, being subjected to physical violence at the hands of those who hate gay people, or being judged.

> ### Why do gay people feel they have to tell anybody?
> ### Why can't they keep it to themselves?

Most gay and lesbian people keep their sexual orientation to themselves, and the price of keeping the secret can be high, whether it is counted in the disproportionate number of gay and lesbian teens who kill themselves or in the higher rate of alcoholism and drug abuse among gay people. There are also, of course, many gay men and women who are comfortable with and accustomed to keeping their homosexuality hidden.

Those gay and lesbian people who choose to tell their friends, family, and colleagues about their sexual orientation do so for many reasons. However, they do it primarily because they want to be themselves, because they want to be honest with those they love and trust, and because it can be difficult, exhausting, and personally destructive to pretend to be someone you're not.

Imagine for a moment what it's like to "keep it to yourself." It's Monday morning at the office, and one of your colleagues asks you what you did for the weekend. You answer, as you always do, "Nothing much," even though you spent the weekend at the hospital with your seriously ill spouse. You could have said that you spent the weekend in the hospital with a person close to you, but more questions would inevitably follow, and ultimately it would be impossible to hide the truth. So to protect your secret, you almost never honestly respond to an innocent question or comment, whether the question is asked by a colleague, a relative, or even a cab driver. You have to monitor everything you say.

As a test, just take note during an average day of how many times your personal life comes up in conversation, whether you're at a mall buying clothes or stuck on the phone with a telephone salesperson. Imagine how you would respond if you had to hide your life. If you were a gay man in a long-term relationship and a telephone salesperson called and asked for the "woman of the house," how would you answer? Would you say, "We're not interested," and hang up? Or would you say, "I'm a man and so is my spouse, so there is no 'woman of the house.'" Or you could do what a friend of mine does who has gotten so fed up with telemarketers that instead of simply saying there's no woman in the house, he answers in his deep, resonant, unmistakably male voice, "You're talking to her."

> **Heterosexuals don't have to come out. Why do gay people?**

Nongay people don't have to come out of the closet because they've never been in it. Growing up, heterosexual boys and girls think nothing of talking about a crush on a friend, rock star, or favorite actor or actress. When they're old enough to date, they can introduce their opposite-gender date to their friends and parents, and they can hold hands walking down the street. At work, they can speak freely about their girlfriend, boyfriend, husband, or wife without fear of losing their job. They can put a picture of a spouse on their desk with no questions asked. They have no need to let people know in a specific way what their sexual orientation is, because their actions and words over time let everyone know they're heterosexual.

Most gay and lesbian people grow up hiding their thoughts, crushes, and relationships. Typically they enter late adolescence or young adulthood with the closely held secret that they're gay or lesbian. Some have gone to great lengths to hide their secret, perhaps going on dates with opposite-gender partners or even marrying. Eventually, many gay men and women choose to reveal the truth about their sexual orientation, but because they've kept that part of their lives secret until that point, disclosure occurs all at once and may come as a shock to friends and loved ones.

I look forward to the day when kids growing up feel no need to hide their true feelings, a day when gay and lesbian kids have no need to come out of the closet because they've never been in it.

> **Why do people choose to come out of the closet to their parents?**
> **Why do gay and lesbian people choose not to come out to their parents?**

People choose to tell their parents they're gay or decide not to tell them for all the reasons gay people generally have for coming out or not coming out. But the decision to tell or not tell parents is often more emotionally profound and complex than is the decision to come out to friends and colleagues.

Michelle, an accountant in her late twenties who lives in Atlanta, finally told her parents she was a lesbian after thinking about doing it for nearly ten years. "At first I couldn't get past the fear they would reject me," she said. "When I was still living at home, I thought they'd throw me out of the house. Then I was afraid they'd pull me out of college. After college I was still afraid they would reject me, but that was compounded by my fear that I'd disappoint them; they had always been so proud of my accomplishments. I never liked keeping secrets from them, but I didn't find it terribly difficult as long as I wasn't dating anyone. But then I fell in love and began a serious relationship. There was so much I wanted to tell my parents, but all we wound up talking about was the weather and the cows (my parents are dairy farmers). I knew they were worried about me being alone, but if I told them I wasn't alone and that my roommate was my lover, I was afraid of destroying their lives. Finally I got up my courage to tell them. It was so hard to say the words, but it was an incredible relief to finally have it out in the open. That was several years ago now, and my parents are doing okay. It's not easy for them to talk about it, but they're making a good effort."

Steve, like many people who choose not to come out to their parents, doesn't see any reason why he should discuss the fact that he's gay with his parents. "I'm nearly forty," he said, "and I've never discussed anything personal with them about any aspect of my life, so why would I talk about this? Besides, they live halfway across the country, so I only see them once or twice a year. Why make trouble, why burden them, when it won't accomplish anything?" Steve resents the pressure some of his friends have put on him to tell his parents the truth: "It's my choice, and it works for me. There's no law that says I have to come out to them if I don't want to. If I thought it would make my life better, I'd think about it. Some of my friends say I would have a closer relationship with my parents if I told them, but I don't want a closer relationship with them."

> How do gay people come out of the closet?

There are many different ways to let people know you're gay. Some people write letters to their parents or friends, discuss it by phone, or come out face-to-face in conversation. Others drop hints, hoping that someone will ask a question that will give them an opportunity to answer truthfully. Still others, celebrities in particular, come out in their published autobiographies, go on television talk shows, or talk about their sexual orientation in a magazine interview. Whatever the choice, the decision to come out is likely one that a gay or lesbian person has thought about and probably agonized over for a very long time.

In general, coming out is not something you do just once and then forget about. For gay and lesbian people who choose to live out of the closet, coming out is something you may do almost every day. There are all kinds of chance encounters and conversations that force gay people to decide whether to answer honestly or not. For example, several years ago, when I was single, I sat down next to a woman on a train from New York to Washington, and within minutes she asked me if I was married. I said that I wasn't. She then asked if I had a girlfriend. I said that I didn't, and she asked if I would be interested in meeting her sister. I could have just said no, and left it at that, but the truth was, because I'm gay, it would have been an inappropriate match. So I told her that I was flattered, but that I was gay. Then she asked if I would be interested in meeting her boss, who was gay, single, and about my age.

Not every gay and lesbian person has to say anything to let people know that he or she is gay. Dave and Judy, best friends and neighbors for more than ten years, told me they never have to tell anyone that they're gay. "We couldn't pass for straight in this lifetime," said Judy, "no matter how hard we tried. We're living proof that the gay stereotype came from somewhere." Dave is very slight, has delicate features, and is extremely effeminate. Judy is a self-described "big butch." She's built like a construction worker, is partial to jeans and sweatshirts, and has a very deep voice. "We're always getting harassed," said Dave, "because people can tell. Sometimes we envy people who can pass, but in a lot of ways it's easier for us. Because we can't hide, we've never had to worry about coming out. We were out before we even knew what we were."

❯ What's it like to come out of the closet?

When Gary, who grew up in a very small southwestern town, came out of the closet to his family, friends, and colleagues on a national television talk show, he felt an incredible sense of relief and renewal. "It was like being born," he said. "The burden had been lifted from my shoulders. For the first time I felt like I had a life. It was the first time I stood up and said, 'This is who I am, and I'm proud of who I am.' For someone who was always embarrassed about being gay, that wasn't easy, especially on national television. And it took me until I was thirty-five to do it. But it was important for me to do it for myself and to set an example for young people, to show them there's a better way, that you don't have to hide the way I did and waste all those years. My only regret about the whole experience was that I hadn't done it sooner. Of course, I felt bad about upsetting my parents, but it'd been on my shoulders since I was a kid. It was time for them to deal with it. It wasn't my problem anymore."

I can't speak for all gay and lesbian people, but virtually all of the hundreds of gay men and lesbians I've interviewed over the years have told me that coming out has ultimately been a positive experience. And that group includes people who have lost their jobs or been rejected by their families and even their children. The experience may have been painful, traumatic, frightening, and overwhelming, but none of the people I've spoken with have said they regret living life free of the closet.

> **When do gay and lesbian people come out of the closet?**

I know a woman who told her parents that she wanted to marry another girl when she was seven years old. I don't know if you would call this coming out of the closet, but she certainly alarmed her parents. And I know a man who didn't tell another soul he was gay until he was nearly eighty-five. More typically, those gay and lesbian people who choose to come out start sharing the truth about their sexual orientation with friends and family from their late teens through their twenties.

> **If my child comes out to me, what should I say?**

See chapter 4, "Family and Children."

> **If my brother comes out to me, does that mean I will be a gay man, too?**
> **If my sister comes out to me, does that mean I will be a lesbian, too?**

No, but it may make you question your own sexuality. This is a perfectly natural response. If, however, you are gay or lesbian, this would be an ideal time to let your sibling know that he or she is not the only one in the family.

❯ Why do closeted gay and lesbian spouses come out of the closet after years or decades of heterosexul marriage?

This question came to me from a woman whose husband came out to her after twenty-five years of marriage. She could not understand why her husband didn't tell her sooner or keep the secret until he died.

From having interviewed men and women who came out after many years of marriage, I know that the decision to come out to a heterosexual spouse is an extremely difficult one and is done because the gay spouse can no longer keep the secret. There can be many reasons for this. For example, they've fallen in love with someone of the same gender, they don't have the strength to keep living with such a large secret, or they want the freedom to find a same-gender partner.

For more information on this subject, see chapter 6, "Relationships and Marriage"; I also suggest reading *The Other Side of the Closet*, a book about the coming-out crisis for heterosexual spouses of gay and lesbian people, by Amity Pierce Buxton.

❯ Why do gay people have to flaunt it?

Several years back, my uncle said to me, "Okay, I can understand wanting to be truthful about who you are, but why do gays have to flaunt it all the time?" When he asked that question, my uncle and I were sitting on beach chairs just a few feet away from the picnic table where my uncle's mother-in-law was playing Scrabble with my friends David and Irene, who were just a couple of months away from being married. At that moment, David was stroking Irene's back in a very tender and loving way. I called my uncle's attention to the obvious public display of affection—David and Irene were clearly flaunting their heterosexuality—and asked my uncle if he considered what David was doing with Irene "flaunting." He got my point.

What we generally consider normal behavior for heterosexual people—talking about a romantic interest or relationship, an affectionate peck on the cheek between husband and wife, holding hands in public, or stroking the back of your beloved—we call "flaunting" when gay and lesbian people do it.

Most gay people, like heterosexual people, have no desire to make a spectacle of themselves. They just want to be themselves in the same way that heterosexual people are. Many times I've heard lesbian and gay people say—and I've said it, too—how wonderful it would be to hold hands when walking down the street with a boyfriend, girlfriend, or spouse without having to worry that someone was going to call you names or come at you with a baseball bat.

> *Why do gay activists urge gay men and lesbians to come out?*

This call to come out is not universal. There are many people who must, because of work or family circumstances, continue to hide their sexual orientation, at least selectively. But for those who can do so without endangering their jobs or getting thrown out of the house, for example, there are a number of reasons to come out, as activists have pointed out.

First, these activists know from personal experience that gay and lesbian people who are living in the closet will feel better about themselves and their lives once they are free of the closet. Second, they believe—as I do—that one-on-one visibility is the key to securing widespread acceptance and equal rights under the law.

For years, surveys have demonstrated that those heterosexuals who know gay people—friends, colleagues, and loved

MONTROSE LIBRARY DISTRICT
320 So. 2nd St.
Montrose, CO 81401

ones—are far more likely to think positively about gay men and lesbians and to support gay rights issues, such as the passage of federal antidiscrimination legislation. But those heterosexuals who don't know any gay men or lesbians—or at least don't know that they know them—are more likely to accept the negative stereotypes and myths so many people grow up believing.

> ### What is National Coming Out Day?

National Coming Out Day, which has been celebrated every October 11 since 1988, commemorates the October 11, 1987, gay and lesbian rights march on Washington, D.C. The annual celebration is sponsored by the Human Rights Campaign, a national political organization that champions gay and lesbian rights issues.

National Coming Out Day is a visibility campaign that encourages lesbian, gay, and bisexual Americans to come out of the closet with pride every day. The idea behind National Coming Out Day is for people to tell the truth about their lives—to come out of the closet—in order to put to rest the myths that society has used against gay, lesbian, and bisexual people.

National Coming Out Day is now marked by events in places all over the world, including New Zealand, India, Thailand, Great Britain, Canada, and Siberia. For example, some communities raise money to place ads in local city newspapers that list the names of people who have decided to come out of the closet. One group in Denver, Colorado, paid for five billboards that said, "Coming Out Means Telling the Truth About Your Life, a Real Family Value." Another group in Philadelphia holds its annual block party every October 11.

MONTROSE LIBRARY DISTRICT
320 So. 2nd St.
Montrose, CO 81401

4

?

FAMILY AND CHILDREN

> *What constitutes a gay or lesbian family?*

Leslie and Joanna and their infant daughter, Emily, are a family.
David and Edward, who just celebrated their twenty-fifth anniversary as a couple, are a family. Al, who divorced his wife
because he is gay, and his two teenage sons who live with him
full-time are a family. Evelyn, a retired math teacher, and three
of her friends, all lesbians, who share a large home on Cape
Cod are a family. These families may not meet the 1950s fan-
tasy *Ozzie and Harriet* model of family life, but then no family
does (and that includes the real-life Ozzie and Harriet). What
these families *do* have is what all families ought to have: love,
care, concern, and commitment to the health, happiness, and
well-being of each family member.

> *Are gay and lesbian people antifamily?*
> *Are gay and lesbian rights groups trying to destroy the American family?*

Despite what some antigay activists have said, gay and lesbian people and gay and lesbian rights organizations do not want to destroy America's family values or the American family—especially since most of us share these same family values and value our place in the lives of our families. And for that matter, why would any group of people or any organization set as its goal the destruction of family life (especially since so many families seem to be doing such a good job of destroying themselves without anyone's help)?

What most gay and lesbian people would like is to be accepted by their families as full and equal members; they would like the definition of family to be broadened to include the realities of American family life—a reality that includes gay and lesbian families of all kinds; and they would like their relationships with their same-gender partners to be protected by law in the same way that heterosexual married couples are protected.

> **How do parents react to a gay or lesbian child?**

How parents react to a lesbian daughter or gay son has a lot to do with who the parents are: their backgrounds, the communities they come from, their ethnic or racial groups, whether or not they are deeply religious, and so forth. But no matter how open-minded parents are—even if half their friends are gay, or they already have one gay child, or they are actively involved in working for gay rights—parents are almost universally upset when they find out their son or daughter is gay.

Parents are likely to have a range of reactions, including shock, tears, denial, disappointment, guilt, and quite possibly anger and hostility. They may hope that this is just a phase, they may wonder what they did wrong, they may express concern about AIDS, they may think that this is an attempt to punish them in some way, or they may be upset that a gay child has chosen to keep them in the dark for so long. Their reactions may have nothing to do with reality, but when it comes to facing the fact that a child is gay or lesbian, many parents react based on the myths and stereotypes we all grew up with. And for parents with strong traditional or fundamentalist religious beliefs, the discovery that a child is gay can lead to enormous conflicts between what their religion tells them about gay people and what they know of their own child.

Many parents, though upset by the news that a child is gay or lesbian, manage to deal with it in a loving way. Andrea's mother and father reacted to the news that she was a lesbian with tears. "They weren't the only ones crying," said Andrea, who said she is closer to her parents now than before she came out to them. "There was a lot they didn't understand, and I know this isn't what they wanted for me, but as much as they were hurting, they managed to tell me that I was their daughter and they loved me. There are still times when it isn't easy. Like the first time I brought my girlfriend home for dinner, they were really nervous. But, then, Penny and I were really nervous, too."

Not all parents who react with tears go on to state their love for their gay or lesbian child. Karen, a junior high school teacher, also cried when her twenty-seven-year-old son, Alex, told her that he was gay, but she had no reassuring words for him, because her tears weren't about her concern for her son, or even tears of disappointment. Karen was crying because she felt betrayed and was furious: "I wanted him dead, and I told him so. As far as I was concerned he was dead. He was out of my life." To Karen, the son she had known died in that moment of revelation. And she was not at all happy with her "new" son.

As strong as Karen's reaction was, some parents react far more harshly. Kevin was seventeen and still living with his parents when they found out he was gay. "I didn't tell them, because I knew they'd flip out," he said. "They're totally into the church, so to them being gay is the most incredibly sinful thing you can do. But I guess they suspected something, because they searched my room and found this note from my boyfriend. You should have seen the look on my father's face when I got home from school. I thought he would kill me." In fact, Kevin's father almost broke Kevin's arm before throwing him out of the house. In the year since then, despite several attempts on his part to contact his parents, Kevin's mother and father have refused to have anything to do with him.

Fortunately, Alex's and Kevin's experiences are not universal. And in Alex's case, after six months his mother began calling almost every day asking him to forgive her and to come home for Thanksgiving.

What is often hardest for parents of a gay or lesbian child to cope with is a sense of embarrassment and/or fear of what friends, neighbors, relatives, or even strangers will think if they find out. Paradoxically, though a gay son or lesbian daughter who comes out of the closet is now free of the burden of hiding the truth, parents most often find themselves in a closet of their own, hiding the truth about their gay or lesbian child. Every time they're faced with a question like "Is your son married?" or "Is your daughter dating anyone?" parents have to decide what to say.

In the few years since Alex came out to her, Karen has told several of her friends and a handful of colleagues that he is gay. All, thus far, have been supportive, but she's still having a hard time. "Hardly a day goes by when one of the other teachers doesn't come bouncing into school talking about a new grandchild," she said. "'Don't worry, this will happen to you soon,' they tell me. I used to run out to the bathroom and cry. Others say, 'The worst thing that could happen would be if my child were a homosexual.' I don't want their pity or rejection. I know I shouldn't feel this way. I should grow up, but that's how I feel. And I'm terrified of having my students find out. Almost every day they call each other 'fag.' Of course I feel compelled to scold them. If only they knew."

For my own mother, it was years before she felt comfortable telling the full truth about me. "I know a lot of parents feel they did something wrong," she told me, "and that people will blame them for raising a gay child, so they don't say anything because they fear being judged. But that wasn't the case with me. I was disappointed and confused, but I still didn't want anyone to know. I felt that if anyone knew, then you would be stigmatized, rejected, looked at as defective or inferior. Somehow I couldn't bear the thought of someone judging you. Before I knew you were gay, I always thought of you as someone very special. After I knew, I didn't see how you could have a full life, how you could be anything but an outsider. You were no longer the son I knew. I don't know if I was ashamed, but I was no longer proud of you."

Years later, after my mother realized I was not defective and was the same son that I was before, she grew more accustomed to answering truthfully, but the reactions people had were nonetheless embarrassing and upsetting. She told me: "When your first book [The Male Couple's Guide] was published, I brought it to a family dinner. I was very proud and wanted to show it to those who were present. I started to speak about the book, but before I said what it was about, some relatives at the table asked to see it, and when it came into their hands, they looked at it, never said a word, and changed the subject. It was as if someone smacked me in the face. I realized that for some people it wasn't even a subject to be spoken about."

My mom sees that family dinner as her turning point: "After that, I refused to hide you. If I spoke about my children, I had to speak about all my children, their lives, the fact that two were married, and that one was gay and in a relationship; otherwise I would have been ashamed of myself for hiding. Parents who are still ashamed of their gay and lesbian children need to look at why they're not questioning what they've been told by society. Most of our children are healthy, decent, caring, sensitive people, and we fail them when we join the rest of society in denying who they are. We are their parents. If we don't defend their right to live full lives, who will?"

> **Do mothers and fathers react differently from each other to a gay or lesbian child?**

Mothers and fathers may react differently to a gay or lesbian child, but not consistently enough to generalize that fathers always have more trouble with their gay sons or that mothers always have more trouble with their lesbian daughters. It is safe to say, however, that mothers and fathers often have different expectations for their children depending on whether that child is a boy or a girl, and that their reactions to a child's homosexuality may be tied to these differing expectations. For example, one father I spoke with who has two gay sons and one nongay son said, "Fathers train males to be macho. So being a 'he-man' is a very important thing. Fathers may expect to live their lack of success in that area through their children. I think with a gay son you may find more disappointment from the father at first. I don't think you find that as much in a mother."

> **If my child comes out to me, what should I say?**
> **What should you do if you think your child is gay?**
> **What should you do if you find out that your child is gay?**

Ideally, if your child is gay or lesbian you will have recognized this fact and educated yourself about gay and lesbian people and discussed the issue with your son or daughter before your child sits you down one day to tell you that he or she is gay. That's in an ideal world.

When a child comes out, what he or she is generally looking for is reassurance. So there are things he or she will be hoping to hear from his or her parents. Ideally, you'll say, "Thank you for telling us. We love you. Knowing that you're gay doesn't change that." A child might also welcome hearing "It must have been very difficult keeping this secret from us." Or "We wish we had known sooner so that we could have been of help to you. How can we be of help to you now?"

There are things that are better left unsaid to a child who has just come out. Don't talk about how devastated you are. Don't talk about your disappointment. Don't ask your child if he or she is sure. Don't suggest that it's just a phase or something that can be cured.

This is one of those moments in your life as a parent when your child needs you to be a parent first, and that means first and foremost taking care of the needs of your child. You can deal with your own issues in private. Your child will likely help you learn what you need to know, but that first discussion should be about your child, not you.

Of course, no two families are alike, so no two situations are exactly alike, which means that there's no one way to deal with the news that a child is gay or lesbian. So if you think your child is gay or lesbian, or if you've recently found out, you need to find the appropriate way to handle your specific circumstances. That means talking to other parents who have gay kids and reading whatever useful material you can get your hands on. The best place to start is with the local chapter of the Federation of Parents, Families and Friends of Lesbians and Gays (PFLAG), where you can talk with other parents who have gay and lesbian children and can get personal, specific advice on what to do in your situation. To find your local chapter and to request printed information, contact PFLAG's national headquarters (see "Resources").

> ### How do grandparents react to a gay grandchild?

"Whatever you do, don't tell the grandparents!" "They're old. They'll never understand. They don't need to know. Let them die in peace." "You're their favorite. Why destroy their image of you?" These are the kinds of exhortations from well-meaning family members that many gay and lesbian people confront when they bring up the possibility of sharing the truth about their lives with the grandparents. And though the grandparents, like the parents, are likely to greet the news of a gay grandchild with surprise, grandparents often prove to be more resilient and more accepting than parents for all the same reasons grandparents are almost always more accepting of what their grandchildren do than of what their own children do.

Bob and Elaine, who are active members of their local PFLAG chapter, told me my favorite story involving grandparents. Bob waited until a couple of years after his son came out to talk with his own parents—the grandparents—about his son's homosexuality: "I went to visit them at home and told them I had something to talk to them about. My mother asked if there was anything wrong. I told her that nothing was wrong but there was something I wanted to talk to them about. So I said, 'You know all those Sundays when you wanted to come visit or you wanted Elaine and me to come here, and I said I had business appointments? We never had business appointments. Elaine and I are members of an organization, and we go to meetings. The organization is for parents of gays.' I stopped at that point, but they didn't react. So I asked, 'Do you know what 'gay' is, Mom?' And my mother looked at me. 'Sure, that's when a guy likes a guy.' And I added, 'Yeah, and when a girl likes a girl.' 'Oh,' she said, 'the girls do it, too?'

"So I proceeded to explain homosexuality. They said, 'That's fine.' And I said, 'The reason we go to the meetings is that one of our sons is gay.' My mother said, 'Oh, we've known that for a long time.' I looked at them, and my mouth fell open in awe. So I asked her which of my sons they thought was gay. And they said Jonathan. I said, 'You're right, but what made you think Jonathan was gay?' 'Well,' my mother said, 'when he talks his voice squeaks, and he uses his hands a lot when he talks.' I said, 'Mom, that has nothing to do with being gay.' I explained a bit more, and at some point they commented, 'They're entitled to everything in life just like everyone else.'"

Not all grandparents are as matter-of-fact, but it's important to remember that grandparents are not nearly as fragile, uninformed, or unwilling to learn about new things as we may think.

When it came time to tell my own grandmother, my family was less than enthusiastic, but I was concerned that she would find out anyway because I was about to have my first book published. More important, I wanted to know that my grandmother would still love me if she knew the truth and I wanted to be able to talk to her about something other than the weather. Because I couldn't discuss my work or my relationship with her, there wasn't a lot to say when we got together or talked by phone. I wrote about my experience with my grandmother in an article for *Newsweek*, which is posted on my Web site at www.ericmarcus.com.

> ### What should you tell a child who has a gay uncle or aunt?

What you say depends on the age of the child, the circumstances, and the questions a child asks. For example, David has a young niece and nephew. He's been with his partner, Kevin, since before the children were born. "From the time they could speak," said David, "they called us Uncle David and Uncle Kevin. To them it seemed like the most natural thing in the world. I'm sure that when they get older and notice that most couples are male and female, they'll have some questions about their two uncles. I've already talked with my brother and sister-in-law about this, and they plan to say that sometimes two men love each other just like Mommy and Daddy love each other. I don't think the kids will have any problem with that. The problems may come up later when they start hearing things about 'fags' at school. But we'll deal with that when the time comes."

> ### Do gay people want to have children?

Like heterosexual people, many gay and lesbian people want to be parents, and for all the same reasons. For example, David and Kevin knew they wanted to be parents even before they met. "I come from a large, happy family," said David. "Early on I saw the importance of being in a family environment. Since my nephew and niece were born and since many of my friends have had children, I've seen how emotionally rewarding it can be. And as I've gotten older, my paternal instincts have gotten very strong." David and Kevin are still exploring their options for having children.

Cynthia and Helen, who have two children, both through artificial insemination, knew from the start of their relationship that children were a part of their long-term plan. "When I pictured what my life would be like," Helen explained, "the picture always included kids. That never changed, even after I realized I was a lesbian. I just knew that I had to find a partner who felt the same way. I made very clear to Cynthia when we first started seeing each other that I wanted children, and fortunately she felt the same way I did. Well, maybe not exactly the same, but by the time we actually did it, Cynthia was just as committed and enthusiastic as I was."

Of course, not all gay people want children, and most often their reasons are the same as those of nongay people who choose not to have children. But there are differences. For example, there are legal issues, such as the difficulty—and in some places the impossibility—of gay or lesbian people adopting a child. And there may also be concerns over how the child of a gay couple will be treated by his or her peers.

> **Do gay and lesbian people have children? How can they?**
> **Can gay and lesbian people, or couples, adopt?**

Many gay men and lesbians have children, although most gay people who are parents became parents while they were involved in heterosexual marriages. However, a growing number of gay people, particularly lesbian couples, are choosing to have children through a variety of methods, including artificial insemination, adoption, co-parenting, and surrogacy. Because two people of the same gender can't accidentally get pregnant, the decision to have children is inevitably one that involves considerable thought and effort.

For single lesbians and lesbian couples, the most popular way to have a child has been through artificial insemination, using either sperm from an anonymous donor or sperm from a known donor. Gay men and male couples most often go the adoption route, although both New Hampshire and Florida expressly bar adoptions by gay men and lesbians (as of early 1999).

Some gay and lesbian people have also chosen to have children through surrogacy or co-parenting arrangements. In its simplest terms, surrogacy involves a man contracting with a woman to have a baby using his sperm. Following the birth of the child, the birth mother gives up her rights to the child. Co-parenting can involve two to four parents. For example, a lesbian couple and a male couple may arrange for one of the men to donate his sperm to impregnate one of the women. The four parents then share custody of the child according to whatever agreement they've worked out. Both of these methods for having children require, among other things, very sound legal advice and detailed contracts.

For gay and lesbian couples, the most significant problem with most of these methods is the issue of legal custody. For example, no state, with the exception of New Jersey (as of early 1999), allows unmarried couples to jointly adopt a child. For a gay or lesbian couple who choose to adopt a child, that means a costly and time-consuming process whereby one partner adopts the child first and then later, in a separate legal proceeding, the other partner adopts the child. For lesbian couples who use artificial insemination or male couples who use surrogacy, once the child is born, the nonbiological partner can apply to adopt the child as the child's second parent.

Because of the expense and potential complexity of completing a "second parent" adoption (or the illegality of gay adoption in New Hampshire and Florida), many gay and lesbian couples find themselves in circumstances where only one of the two parents has legal rights to the couple's child or children. In the event that the adoptive father or biological mother dies or the couple separates, in these cases the second parent has no legal claim as the parent of the child or children. And that's when the legal nightmare really begins.

> *Why do some people object to gay men and women having children?*
> *Do gay parents raise gay children?*

The common myths about gay and lesbian parents—and I emphasize the word *myths*—that are often expressed by those who oppose gay and lesbian people having, adopting, and raising children are that they are more likely to molest their children, that they will raise gay and lesbian children, that children raised by two parents of the same gender will be poorly adjusted, and that the children of gay parents will automatically be discriminated against.

First, gay and lesbian people are no more likely to sexually abuse their children than heterosexual people (and as the study cited in chapter 1 from the Children's Hospital in Denver suggests, gay and lesbian parents are far less likely to do so). Second, you cannot intentionally raise a gay child any more than you can intentionally raise a heterosexual child. From everything that is known, a parent cannot affect a child's sexual orientation. Third, whether or not a child is well adjusted has more to do with whether or not the child is loved than whether there are two mothers, two fathers, a mother and a father, or a single parent.

The one argument against gay and lesbian people raising children that is based in fact is that the children of gay and lesbian people are likely to face special challenges because of society's prejudice against gay men and lesbians. It is true that the children of gay and lesbian people may feel they have to hide the fact that their parents are gay or may have to contend with prejudiced remarks or negative reactions from their friends or the parents of their friends who don't approve of gay and lesbian people. But this is no more a rational argument against gay and lesbian people having children than it would be for any other group that faces discrimination in our society. This is, however, a good argument for working to change people's negative attitudes.

> *What happens when gay or lesbian couples who have kids split up?*
> *Who gets the children?*
> *Are there visitation rights?*
> *What happens when one parent dies?*

Many gay and lesbian couples, like heterosexual couples, split up. And when children are involved it can be especially complicated, because for gay and lesbian couples who have kids, often only one parent is the legal parent (adoptive or biological).

When gay and lesbian couples in this situation can agree on custody arrangements—which, ideally, they have put into writing prior to having the child—then there are no problems beyond the usual challenges divorced couples with children face. But when a gay or lesbian couple who have a child can't agree on custody arrangements, and only one parent is the legal parent, then the other parent will likely find that he or she has no legal rights.

For couples in which both parents are legal parents—that is, both have legally adopted the child, or one is the biological parent and the other is a legal adoptive parent—there is plenty of legal precedent to be followed should the parents be unable to agree on custody arrangements.

In the event that a parent dies, the surviving parent will retain custody of the child or children as long as that parent is the biological or a legal adoptive parent. If the surviving partner is not the biological or a legal adoptive parent, the outcome can be disastrous, because in the eyes of the law that parent has no legal relationship with the child. If the second parent wishes to gain custody of the child or children, he or she will face a difficult legal battle to gain custody, particularly if the child's or children's legal next of kin wishes to assume custody.

> **Is it better to tell children about a homosexual parent or hide the truth?**
> **What's the best time to tell children?**

I believe that if it's at all possible, it's best to be honest about your homosexuality with your children. I think that family secrets are poison, whatever their nature. But that's my opinion. I've talked to parents who insist that I'm right, and I've talked to parents who insist that I'm wrong and that it's none of my business.

Sometimes parents keep their homosexuality a secret from their children out of necessity. If a parent is embroiled in a custody battle in which the sexual orientation of the parent could affect the outcome, then hiding the truth is essential. For parents who are not faced with this kind of dilemma, whether or not they share this information with their children is a matter of personal choice.

What parents choose to do depends on many things, including their specific circumstances. For example, if an openly gay male couple or lesbian couple is raising a child together from infancy, they are not likely to hide the nature of their relationship from their child and will therefore have nothing to disclose. The child will have observed her parents as a couple—being affectionate, sharing a bed—and will over time become aware that they are gay or lesbian.

For a parent who has left a heterosexual marriage, it's a matter of deciding whether or not to tell a child that the parent is something different from what he thought he was. If the gay or lesbian parent has custody of that child, it could be very difficult to hide the truth, especially if the parent is actively dating or has a new partner. Kids aren't stupid, and if there's a secret to be found out, they'll make every effort to uncover the truth. If, on the other hand, the parent does not have custody and the child visits only during designated times, it is easier to hide the truth.

For those parents who choose to come out to their children, the rule of thumb is: the sooner the better. That was what Lloyd, a father of a teenage son and daughter, learned from other gay fathers he met through a local support group: "I found out that the younger the children, the easier it was—especially before they were teens and dealing with their own sexuality and were more aware about sexual things and had peer pressure. When they're younger, they're more accepting of things. They're not even so sure what 'gay' is. They just want to know that their father is still their father."

Joy Schulenburg, a lesbian mom and the author of *Gay Parenting*, concurs that children deal better with the news that a parent is gay when they're still young: "Among the children I talked to and corresponded with, there were distinct differences in attitudes between those who had been under twelve when they learned their parent was gay and those who had been twelve and over. The under-twelve age group seemed largely indifferent to their parent's sexual orientation (which is true also of children of heterosexuals). Most of them simply didn't understand what all the fuss was about. Parents were loved because they were parents, despite any personal quirks and without reservations. Once puberty set in, with its sexual awakening and attending social pressures, reactions varied and the incidence of concern and initial rejection increased."

❯ How do children react to gay parents?

How children react to a parent's sexual orientation depends to a large degree on when they find out a parent is gay. For a child who has been raised since birth or early childhood by two parents of the same gender, the awareness is evolutionary. At first the child may be aware only that she has two parents of the same gender who sleep in the same bed. Eventually she will realize that most of her friends have parents of the opposite gender and will likely ask her parents why she has two daddies or two mommies instead of a mommy and a daddy. Then she'll learn the words that designate her parents' sexual orientation and gain a fuller understanding of what this means. For a child like this, there is no one moment of revelation when she discovers that her supposedly heterosexual parent is gay. So for this child there is no real news to react to.

When children are raised by a mother and father, and later one of the parents comes out of the closet, children react in a variety of ways, from shock and rejection to relief that their parent has finally confirmed what they already knew. Children may also be concerned about the possibility of a gay father contracting AIDS.

Some parents have had terrible experiences, like one woman I know whose devoutly religious teenage daughter refused to ever see her again. Other parents have had very positive experiences, like a man I know whose two sons just wanted to be certain that their father still loved them. Lloyd, the father of two children, said that what he learned from his own experience and the experiences of other gay fathers he knows was that "in almost all cases when the kids found out, it was okay. This was their father; he was gay. They would have some problems but would eventually come around."

Tina, who has been a stepmother to her partner's two sons, concluded from her experience that the way children ultimately respond to their parents' homosexuality has a great deal to do with the kind of relationship the parents have with their children: "The secret really turns out to be, do you have a loving relationship with your kids? And if you love and respect them, they tend to love and respect you. It's something that needs a lot of attention and work and commitment, like any relationship."

> *What kinds of special problems do children of gay parents have?*

The world is not always a very friendly place for gay and lesbian people, and that makes it a challenging place for their children as well. Nonetheless, as reported by Daniel Goleman in the *New York Times* in December 1992, "According to a review of new studies in the current issue of the journal *Child*

Development, children raised by gay parents are no more likely to have psychological problems than those raised in more conventional circumstances. While they may face teasing or even ridicule, especially in adolescence, the studies show that, over all, there are no psychological disadvantages for children . . . being raised by homosexuals."

As reported in the article, one of the studies, which was conducted by Dr. Julie Gottman, a clinical psychologist in Seattle, found that as a group, the children of lesbians did not differ from children of heterosexual mothers in their social adjustment or their identity as a boy or girl. And the children of lesbians were no more likely to be homosexual than those of heterosexual mothers. Dr. Gottman said, "What mattered most for their adjustment was whether the mother had a partner in the home, whether male or female. If so, those children tended to do somewhat better than the others in self-confidence, self-acceptance, and independence. But the sexual orientation of the lesbian mothers had no adverse affects." According to the article, that conclusion "was confirmed by about three dozen studies reviewed in *Child Development* by Charlotte Patterson, a psychologist at the University of Virginia."

❯ *What do kids call their two same-gender parents?*

What may be a perplexing dilemma for an adult who is trying to imagine how a child figures out what to call two mommies or two daddies has been no problem for the kids I've talked to. Susan, who is ten, calls her fathers, who have raised her since birth, Papa Don and Daddy David. Michael, who is twenty-four, calls his natural father Dad and his father's partner, who raised Michael, Mama Chuck. (Mind you, Mama Chuck is over six feet four inches tall and weighs 250 pounds.) Ellen and Doug, who are in their twenties, call their mother Mom and their mother's partner, whom she's been with for the last ten years, by her first name.

> **Is there an organization for gay and lesbian people who have children?**

There are several organizations around the country for gay and lesbian people who have children. One of the oldest is the Family Pride Coalition (formerly GLPCI), an international organization that supports, educates, and advocates for gay, lesbian, bisexual, and transgendered parents and their families. There is also an affiliated organization for the children of these parents, Children of Lesbians and Gays Everywhere (COLAGE) (see "Resources").

5

?

DATING

> *How do gay people meet?*

When Barbara, a clerk-typist from Philadelphia, was a young woman back in the early 1950s, she desperately wanted to meet other women who were gay. Until then, she had only read about lesbians in novels. "I don't remember exactly how I knew about gay bars, probably from all the reading I'd done," she said, "but somehow I heard about a bar in New York City. To save money on bus fare, I hitchhiked to New York from where I lived in Philadelphia—this was obviously a long time ago. When I finally found the place and found my people, it was marvelous. I don't like bars, but I was thrilled to meet people who were like me."

Though these bars were just about the only places gay men and lesbians could go in the 1950s to meet other people like themselves, today in every major and midsize city, gay and lesbian people meet in a variety of settings, from gay and lesbian running clubs and softball teams to religious organizations and volunteer groups—in addition to bars, restaurants, and clubs that cater specifically to a gay and lesbian clientele. Many cities also have gay and lesbian community centers where various organizations meet and events of all kinds are held.

But these aren't the only places gay and lesbian people meet each other or the only ways in which they meet. Just like everyone else, gay and lesbian people meet at work, at social events, on the Internet, and at the grocery store, and are introduced through friends and family. When I was in my early twenties and single, my mother and her friend Fran decided that their gay sons should meet. They figured that if they weren't going to have daughters-in-law of any kind, they might as well try for Jewish sons-in-law. (It was a nice try, but we didn't make it past the second date.)

> *How do gay people spot each other?*

Figuring out if the man or woman you're interested in dating is in fact gay or lesbian is often no small challenge. Unless you meet in a setting where you know for sure that everyone is gay, you're left in the difficult position of trying to figure it out. I remember once in college telling my friend Mary Ann about an upperclassman I had a crush on. Every time I mentioned his name over a period of several days, Mary Ann said, "I don't think he's interested in men." The more Mary Ann tried to dissuade me, the more I insisted that he was gay. Finally, I listed all my reasons for believing that John was gay. I told Mary Ann, "He's sensitive; he seems to enjoy my company; he takes good care of himself. There's just something about him. I know he's gay." Mary Ann rolled her eyes and said, "I'm sure he's not." I asked her how she could be so certain, and she looked at me as if she couldn't believe how dense I was and said, "Because I've been sleeping with him for the past month!"

Sometimes it's relatively easy to figure out if the man or woman you've taken a liking to is gay—for example, if he or she is wearing a button or jewelry that indicates support for gay causes. Another clue might be if his or her style of clothing or haircut conforms to what's popular among gay and lesbian people (although as gay-inspired fashions move quickly into the mainstream, this can lead to some confusion). But if there are no outward signs or the signs are inconclusive, it can be a major challenge. If you're in a business situation, for example, you may have to be very careful, for reasons beyond all the usual ones for being careful about pursuing romantic interests at the office. If you've kept your sexual orientation a secret from your colleagues, you have to feel confident that the person you're interested in is also gay or lesbian—and, in addition, will protect your secret. The last thing you want to do in a case like this is reveal the fact that you're gay to someone who will not be sensitive to your need for secrecy.

When Jane met Justine in the company cafeteria, it was love at first sight, but Jane had no idea whether Justine was gay. She had her hopes, especially when Justine gave her a broad smile when they met, but she couldn't be sure. Over the next couple of weeks Jane gathered evidence from their conversations: "I found out that Justine lived alone. She never talked about boyfriends. Her politics seemed on target. But it wasn't until I met her at her apartment one evening to go to the movies that I was absolutely sure. Her books were a dead giveaway." Of course, Justine was also gathering evidence, so by the time she invited Jane to meet her at her apartment before the movie, she was confident that Jane was also gay: "I could tell from the way she looked at me. Jane may have thought she was being subtle, but if there's one thing Jane isn't, it's subtle!"

> ### What do gay people do on a date?

Whether it's the first date or the tenth, what gay people do on dates varies as much as what heterosexual people do on dates. For example, on my first date with a man, when I was seventeen, my neighbor Bob and I went to see a movie about two young men who had fallen in love. During the movie Bob and I held hands (but I waited for the lights to go down before I searched for Bob's hand because I was afraid of what people might say if they saw what we were doing). Other examples: Scott and Mark had planned to drive to the beach for their fifth date, but they never got out of the house. For Cynthia and Debbie, their first date started with dinner on Debbie's terrace overlooking the Pacific Ocean in Santa Monica.

> ### Who makes the first move? Who drives? Who pays?

Debbie's first date with Cynthia went really well. Dinner was wonderful. There was plenty to talk about. Both were feeling very romantic by the time they had finished dessert and coffee and were standing at the railing of Debbie's terrace watching the sun set over the Pacific. Debbie wanted to kiss Cynthia. And Cynthia wanted to kiss Debbie. "But we were both waiting for the other to make the first move!" explained Debbie. "Both of us were pretty new to dating women, and growing up, you learn that the boy is supposed to make the first move. But finally, after standing there looking at each other for a while, not knowing what to do, we just started laughing because we realized why we were just standing there and not doing what we both wanted to do. So we just went for it. After the first kiss, whoever felt like making the first move did. Well, it wasn't always that simple, but we tried to do what we felt like doing and not what we thought we should do based on the fact that we're women and the roles we're taught to play."

When you're two women or two men in a dating situation, you don't just fall into the standard boy-girl roles, unless you're both comfortable choosing compatible roles. For most gay and lesbian people, who makes the first move, who drives, who pays for the date, who makes the first call, and so forth are dictated by many different factors that are often not nearly as simple and clear-cut as the standard boy-girl routine that heterosexual people can choose to follow. So who pays for dinner may depend on who asked whom out for the date or who makes more money. Or you may agree that you always go dutch. The one who reaches across the table to plant the first kiss may simply be the one who is feeling more confident at a given moment. And the one who drives may be the one who prefers to drive. But, of course, gay people aren't the only ones who face the challenge—and opportunity—of undefined roles. Roles for heterosexuals are not nearly as well defined as they once were.

> **What do you do if you are heterosexual and you think the man or woman you are dating is gay?**

First you have to think about what it is that makes you think the person you're dating is gay or lesbian. My friend Kitty said that some of her friends think that a man is gay if he won't have sex on the first date. She said, "Plenty of straight men don't want to go to bed on the first date. Most often it has nothing to do with whether or not a guy likes women. I don't understand what the rush is. Once you've crossed that line, there's no going back. And it's also possible that the guy you're dating just doesn't find you all that physically interesting. That's a hard one to accept."

But sometimes a lack of interest in sex may indeed be an indicator that your boyfriend or girlfriend is gay or lesbian. If you feel that the man or woman you're dating doesn't have a lot of interest in the opposite gender, you can try asking him or her, "What is the problem?" If you're comfortable, you can ask bluntly, "Are you gay?" but that won't necessarily elicit an honest response. If my first girlfriend in college had asked me if I was gay, I would have said no—not because I was trying to hide anything, but because I hadn't even admitted it to myself. Although Anna never asked me, I learned from her years later that she was pretty sure I was gay because of my lack of interest in doing anything physical other than kissing.

If you can't get what you feel is an honest response from the man or woman you're dating, you may find that your only alternative is to end the dating relationship. That doesn't mean you can't be friends, but there is no reason to subject yourself to a relationship with someone who would really rather be with a person of the same gender.

6

?

RELATIONSHIPS AND MARRIAGE

> **Do gay people have couple relationships?**

Several years ago, I had a talk about relationships with my best friend's dad. We had just come from dinner with my buddy and his male spouse of seven years. We got into a conversation about the ups and downs of long-term relationships, and my friend's dad said, "One of the things I've learned as I've gotten to know gay people is that people are people, love is love, and relationships are relationships, whether it's two men, two women, or a man and a woman."

Because he now knows several gay and lesbian people, including a number of couples, my friend's father has had the opportunity to see that gay and lesbian people have relationships that are full of all the joy, excitement, challenge, and satisfaction, as well as hurt, disappointment, and tragedy, that nongay people experience in their relationships.

> ### How long do gay and lesbian couple relationships last?

Gay and lesbian couple relationships, like heterosexual couple relationships, can last anywhere from a matter of days to a half century or more. But because gay and lesbian people remain largely hidden, there are no accurate statistics on the number of gay and lesbian couples or the average length of these relationships. But I can tell you from the research I did for my book on happy, long-lasting relationships that there are many gay and lesbian couples who have been together for ten, twenty, thirty, or forty years or more.

> ### Are there more gay and lesbian couples now than in years past? Why?

In all likelihood, there are more gay and lesbian couples now than in the past, probably many more, and there are several reasons for this, from changing expectations to more varied opportunities to meet potential partners.

Until recent years, the prevailing myth about gay and lesbian relationships was that they couldn't possibly last. Even though old myths die hard, most gay and lesbian people now know that it's possible to have a relationship, and many actively pursue that possibility.

Finding a potential partner is now easier than it was in the past. First, there are more and more openly gay and lesbian people out there to choose from. Second, there are many more places to meet, from religious groups and professional organizations to softball leagues and the Internet.

Many gay and lesbian couples can now also count on the kind of familial, religious, social, and even legal support that heterosexual couples take for granted. For example, when Brent and Tom gave a party for their tenth anniversary, Brent's parents and sister were an important part of the celebration. "Both sets of parents are very supportive of our relationship," said Brent. "Tom's parents would have been there, but they're quite a bit older than my parents, and the trip was just too much for them. But they called and sent a gift." Tom and Brent have also formalized their relationship with a commitment ceremony at their local church and with a domestic partnership certificate offered by the city of San Francisco to unmarried couples. (For more on domestic partnerships, see "What can gay couples do to achieve rights similar to those granted by marriage laws?" later in this chapter.)

> ### What do gay and lesbian people call their partners?

In one of her first nationally syndicated columns for the *Detroit News*, journalist Deb Price wrote about the problem lesbian and gay people face when introducing a partner, spouse, lover, significant other, special friend, longtime companion, wife, husband, boyfriend, girlfriend, life partner, or whatever. As Price wrote, "Who says the gay rights movement hasn't made a lot of progress? In just 100 years, we've gone from the love that dare not speak its name to the love that doesn't know its name." She asked readers to help her come up with a term that she could use to introduce her partner, Joyce.

The answers Price got weren't all positive. As she wrote in her column a month later: "People who read 'G-A-Y' as 'S-E-X' apparently also misread my question: I didn't ask people to call Joyce names." Price then listed some of the names writers volunteered: "sodomite," "partner in sin," and "sick." Despite the name-calling, most of those who wrote to Price had serious suggestions, the best of which, Price decided, was *love-mate*. Although this seems like a reasonable choice, I have to admit I have never once used *love-mate* to describe my significant other, partner, boyfriend, or spouse.

Whatever words gay and lesbian people use for their "love-mates," they often use different words depending on whom they're talking to. For example, when Donna talks about Joanna with her colleagues or family, she refers to Joanna as her spouse or partner. "These are words straight people can easily relate to, and they know what I mean," said Donna. When she talks about Joanna with her lesbian and gay friends, Donna uses either *lover, wife,* or for fun, *the little woman.* She knows that her gay and lesbian friends know that *lover* means the same thing as *spouse,* and that calling Joanna her "wife" doesn't imply that Donna is the husband. "We're two wives," said Donna. "Gay people know what these words mean because we're used to them, but if I talked to my mother about Joanna being my wife, she would look at me like I was crazy."

Daryl and Carlton, who have been a couple for nearly fifteen years, told me my favorite story on this subject: "When Daryl took me to his architecture school graduation dinner party, he introduced me as his 'comrade' to all his professors. Everyone thought we were communists or something. It was embarrassing. By the end of the night I convinced him to use *spouse.*"

> ### Do gay and lesbian couples have pet names or nicknames for each other?

Like heterosexual couples, gay and lesbian couples over time often develop their own "language." This language—words and phrases that have special meaning only to the individual couple—may include pet names. Over the years I've talked to lesbian and gay people in couple relationships who have affectionately called each other everything from "Bunny" to "Wonkie."

> ### Who plays the husband, and who plays the wife?

When it comes to gay and lesbian relationships, this is the one question I am asked more often than any other. And I've been asked this question by people who are in traditional husband-wife relationships and by young married professionals who have never assumed the roles of husband or wife.

One of the first times I was asked this question was in 1988, when I was working for CBS News. The colleague who asked it was well educated, knew plenty of gay and lesbian people, and didn't have a prejudiced bone in her body. She was just curious and thought I could answer the question. I answered her question with a question. I asked her who in her relationship—she had been married to a man for several years—played the husband and who played the wife. I wasn't trying to be glib or sarcastic. I just wanted her to think about the question and how it related to her own life. She smiled, because she knew what I was getting at, and said, "We don't really have traditional husband-wife roles. We both work. We both cook, although my husband is a better cook. We send out the laundry. And we both hate to clean." I then explained that for the gay and lesbian couples I knew it was pretty much the same. Chores didn't fall along traditional husband-wife lines. For example, who made dinner was far more dependent on who got home from work first than on who was more feminine. As for who, if anyone, took the lead in decision making, that just depended on the individual personalities of the people in the relationship.

Like many heterosexual couples, some gay and lesbian couples follow a more traditional husband-wife model. For example, during the first year after a male couple I know adopted an infant boy, one stayed home and took care of the baby and did the shopping, cleaning, and all the cooking. The other partner went to the office and provided the financial support for the whole family. The next year, they switched roles; the one who had worked at an office came home to take care of the baby, and the one who had been taking care of the baby went back

to working in an office. This isn't the only possible arrange-
ment. For another couple I met, both women had full-time
jobs, but one partner performed the traditional "female"
chores, like cleaning the house and cooking, while the other
partner took care of the traditional "male" chores, such as
mowing the lawn and maintaining the car. It just so happened
that the more outwardly feminine of the two was the one who
took care of the traditional "male" chores.

> **Who brings home flowers?**
> **Who makes the plans to celebrate Valentine's Day?**
> **Who drives?**

Even among my most liberated heterosexual couple friends,
including couples in which the wives have profoundly successful careers, it's the husbands who bring their wives flowers, the husbands who plan something special for Valentine's
Day (or risk being flogged), and the husbands who almost always drive the car.

For gay men and lesbians who are in couple relationships,
unless they assume well-defined husband-wife roles, there is
no falling back on traditional gender roles to figure out who
should be giving whom the flowers and who should be seated
behind the wheel. It just depends on individual expectations
and preferences.

For example, Joel thinks it's important to celebrate Valentine's Day. And so does Tony, his partner of three years. So every
year they've thought up surprises for each other. "The first year,"
explained Tony, "I got home from work early and made a trail of
cut-out hearts from the front door to the bedroom. So when
Joel got home, he followed the trail into the bedroom, where I
was waiting. The candles were set out, I had our favorite CD
playing—you know, the whole business." Tony hadn't forgotten
about the holiday and surprised Joel with two dozen red roses

and a bottle of champagne: "I also had reservations at our favorite restaurant." And what about driving? "I hate to drive, but I'm great at reading maps," said Tony, "and Joel loves to drive, but he never knows where he's going. So it works out well for us."

> **Who plays the husband and who plays the wife in bed?**

For some gay and lesbian couples, one partner routinely takes the passive (or what was traditionally considered the wife's) role and one partner takes the aggressive (or what was traditionally considered the husband's) role. For most gay and lesbian couples, however—and, I suspect, for many heterosexual couples as well—roles aren't so regimented and may shift back and forth between the partners from minute to minute, hour to hour, day to day. (For more on this subject, see chapter 13, "Sex.")

> **What are "butch-femme" relationships?**

According to Lillian Faderman, who has written about the butch-femme lesbian subculture in her book *Odd Girls and Twilight Lovers*, some lesbians, primarily young and working-class lesbians during the 1950s and 1960s, assumed either masculine ("butch") or feminine ("femme") roles. They expressed these roles in their manner of dress, their demeanor, their sexual behavior, and their choice of partner: butches sought femmes, and femmes hoped to attract butches.

Today, while some lesbian couples and some gay male couples may play traditionally masculine and feminine roles, the strict butch-femme role-playing of earlier decades is no longer common.

> **What kinds of relationship problems do gay and lesbian people have that result from being gay?**

All couples, heterosexual and homosexual, face challenges. Gay and lesbian people face some extra challenges, not the least of which is a world that is still fundamentally unwelcoming of same-gender couples. For example, gay and lesbian couples cannot count on the support of family or religious institutions, and gay people are not allowed to legally marry. Besides the legal and financial benefits of marriage, gay and lesbian couples are denied the psychological benefit derived from having their commitment to each other sanctioned and affirmed by the state.

Before gay men and women even get to an age when couple relationships are possible, they have to struggle with their own negative feelings about their sexual orientation (the result of society's general condemnation of homosexuality). And often these feelings are still with them when they enter into a relationship. Add to that society's expectation that gay and lesbian relationships can't possibly last, and the dearth of visible role models, and it begins to seem miraculous that there are any gay and lesbian couples at all.

> *Are male couples monogamous?*
> *Are female couples monogamous?*

I've met many male couples who are monogamous, and others who are not. Anecdotal evidence and a number of studies suggest that male couples are less frequently monogamous than heterosexual couples. On the other hand, I've met plenty of lesbian couples who are monogamous, and very few who are not. Anecdotal evidence and a number of studies suggest that lesbian couples are more frequently monogamous than heterosexual couples.

> *Can gay people legally marry?*

In the United States, no state currently (as of early 1999) permits two people of the same gender to legally marry. However, in a handful of European countries, including Sweden, Denmark, Norway, Spain, Iceland, Belgium, and the Netherlands, gay and lesbian domestic partnerships have been given legal protection that comes close to or matches the legal protections given to married heterosexual couples. In Italy, despite the opposition of the Roman Catholic Church, city governments in Pisa and Florence voted in 1998 to make gay domestic partnerships equal in status to common-law marriage, giving gay and lesbian couples the right to joint insurance and tax returns. And several countries around the world legally recognize same-gender relationships in issues of immigration, including Australia, New Zealand, Canada, the United Kingdom, as well as many of the European countries mentioned above.

> **Can't gay and lesbian couples get married in
> San Francisco and New York City?**

Only states can grant the legal right to marry. However, several cities, including New York and San Francisco, have passed laws allowing nonmarried couples—same gender and opposite gender—to register as "domestic partners." These largely symbolic gestures give nonmarried couples who choose to register their relationships the opportunity to go on record as being a committed couple. But domestic partners are not granted the legal rights that are conferred on legally married couples.

> **Why are gay people fighting for the legal right to get
> married?**
> **What advantages are there to a legal marriage?**

Most gay and lesbian people want the legal right to marry because they want the same legal protections and financial benefits granted to nongay married couples.

The legal protections and benefits of marriage are considerable. In most states, married couples have the legal right to be on each other's insurance and pension plans. Married couples also get special tax exemptions and deductions and are eligible for Social Security survivor's benefits. A married person may inherit property and may have automatic rights of survivorship that avoid inheritance tax. Married couples can routinely adopt a child jointly. And marriage laws offer legal protection in the event that a relationship comes to an end, providing for an orderly distribution of property.

In the case of death or medical emergency, the married spouse is the legal next of kin, which means that he or she can make all decisions regarding medical care and funeral arrangements. And the next of kin is granted automatic visitation rights. The story of Sharon Kowalski and Karen Thompson tragically demonstrated what the lack of these automatic rights means when something goes wrong. After a 1983 car accident, Sharon Kowalski was left brain-damaged and quadriplegic. It took her spouse, Karen Thompson, seven years to be named guardian, over the objections of Kowalski's parents, who said their daughter had never told them she was a lesbian. They also barred Thompson from visiting their daughter's nursing home for several years after the accident. What took Karen Thompson seven years to achieve would have been granted automatically to a legal husband or wife.

For gay and lesbian couples who are raising children, the absence of state-sanctioned marriage can lead to all kinds of legal problems. (For more on this subject, see chapter 4, "Family and Children.")

And finally, there is the kind of dilemma faced by a couple like Charlene, who is a U.S. citizen, and Sandrina, who is French. Shortly after Sandrina arrived in the United States to get her master's degree in English literature, she met Charlene. Following a six-month courtship, they moved in together, hoping they could figure out a way for Sandrina to stay in the United States after she graduated. For a heterosexual couple, marriage would have been a natural solution. If Charlene and Sandrina could marry, then Sandrina would be eligible for citizenship and would be allowed to live and work in the United

States. After exhausting all legal options, Sandrina chose to remain in the United States with Charlene illegally. Both women live in fear that Sandrina will be discovered and deported.

> **Why do people oppose extending legal marriage to gay men and lesbians?**
> **What are their arguments against it?**

People oppose extending legal marriage to gay men and lesbians because of their religious convictions and political views, and because of ignorance and prejudice. Over the years I've heard all kinds of arguments against letting gay people marry: "God created Adam and Eve, not Adam and Steve"; "It will cost too much"; "It will destroy the American family"; "It will devalue heterosexual marriage"; and so on.

Those who base their objections to same-gender marriage on their religious beliefs overlook the fact that we live in a constitutional democracy with a strict separation of church and state, not a Christian state governed by the Bible. So whether God created Adam and Eve, Adam and Steve, or any other combination should have no bearing on state marriage laws.

Regarding the argument that legal marriage for gay men and lesbians would be too costly—that, for example, companies would have to extend health benefits to same-gender partners and the federal government would have to provide Social Security survivor's benefits—perhaps we need first to consider whether we as a nation can afford to extend these benefits to anyone at all, whether heterosexuals, who marry in far greater numbers than gay and lesbian people ever will, or gay men and women.

As far as fears that legal gay marriage will weaken American family life, it seems to me that encouraging stable couple relationships among gay and lesbian people can't help but help strengthen the American family. And the claim that gay marriage will devalue heterosexual marriage presumes that a relationship between two people of the same gender is somehow something less than the real thing, that it's a parody of the heterosexual model. Anyone who has known a long-term gay or lesbian couple knows that this is simply not true.

What I find interesting about some of the antigay marriage rhetoric is that it is coming from the same religious and political leaders and organizations that once condemned gay and lesbian people for failing at relationships and for leading lives of promiscuity. So we're condemned for being single *and* for wanting to get married.

Those who believe that gay men and lesbians should have the right to legally marry, yet fear that it will never be granted, can take heart from the fact that until a 1967 Supreme Court ruling, some states prohibited marriage, sex, or procreation between black people and white people.

> *What can gay couples do to achieve rights similar to those granted by marriage laws?*
> *What about these new domestic partnership laws?*

There are several legal documents that gay and lesbian couples can complete that give them some of the legal rights granted to heterosexual married couples. These include a will; a durable power of attorney, which allows you to designate a particular individual as the person you want to make medical and financial decisions for you should you become incapacitated; and joint ownership agreements. You can also draw up a legal letter, which my attorney calls a *designation of preference*, in which you state, for example, that you want your partner to be the first person to visit you should you be confined to an intensive care unit. A hospital does not have to honor a designation of preference letter, but such a letter, along with the support of your doctor, may just do the trick.

There is another legal document that is being offered by several cities across the country to nonmarried couples, both heterosexual and homosexual. It's called a domestic partnership agreement. In San Francisco, for example, couples who choose to register their relationships with the city through a domestic partnership certificate declare that they have "an intimate, committed relationship of mutual caring," that they live together, and that they agree to be responsible for each other's basic living expenses. Though the domestic partnership certificate is largely symbolic—only states have the right to issue marriage licenses—some couples have attempted to use it to gain family benefits for gay and lesbian spouses from employers, insurance companies, and even health clubs.

> **What kinds of ceremonies do gay and lesbian couples have to celebrate their commitment to each other?**
> **Why do they have such celebrations?**

Although there is no wedding tradition for gay and lesbian couples, that doesn't mean they don't celebrate their commitment to each other. It just means that the range of celebrations is very broad, from a simple exchange of rings in private to a pull-out-all-the-stops event, including a church ceremony, matching tuxedos or dresses, traditional vows, a formal reception for two hundred, and a four-tiered wedding cake topped with two grooms or two brides.

Gay and lesbian couples who choose religious ceremonies are having less and less difficulty in finding ministers or other mainstream religious leaders to officiate, but congregations don't always welcome gay and lesbian commitment ceremonies in their houses of worship, and local ministers are occasionally punished by their superiors for performing such ceremonies.

Leslie and Karen had hoped to hold their ceremony in the church they attended together for five years in San Diego. "But when push came to shove," said Leslie, "the majority of the congregation really didn't want us to do it. Before they made a formal decision, we decided to have the ceremony in our own home. We didn't want anything to spoil what for us was a very, very important and happy occasion."

The decision of various ministers and rabbis to conduct religious union ceremonies for gay and lesbian couples has led to widespread debate as well as well-publicized confrontations across religious denominations.

I attended my first gay commitment ceremony in 1992. The two men, close friends who were both in their late twenties, had been together for nearly three years and formally engaged for a year (they bought each other identical watches for their engagement). The invitation stated that Bill and Henry wanted me to join them for a ceremony celebrating their commitment to each other. The invitation went beyond giving the usual date, place, and time to explain what would happen at the ceremony. "We knew that most of the people we invited had never been to a gay commitment ceremony before," explained Henry. "We thought that the best way to make them comfortable was to spell out in the invitation what to expect. So in the invitation we said there would be an exchange of vows and rings, readings by several different people, and then a reception."

I don't know quite what I expected, but Bill and Henry's ceremony, which they held in their new apartment, was the most moving "wedding" I've ever been to. (I've put *wedding* in quotes because Bill and Henry didn't call it a wedding, but in almost all ways, except for the fact that the two men couldn't get a marriage license, that's what it was.) Bill and Henry conducted the ceremony themselves. They were flanked on either side by their parents. Both stated their love for each other and their mutual commitment before exchanging traditional gold wedding bands. Then Henry's mother and father spoke, as did

Bill's father. By this time I was crying, as were most of the fifty people—friends, family, neighbors, both gay and nongay—packed into Bill and Henry's living room. It was an incredibly emotional and loving ceremony, especially as various friends and family came up to speak. Then we all congratulated the dazed couple and feasted on Chinese food. The next day they left for their honeymoon.

I wasn't quite sold on the importance of a commitment ceremony before I attended Bill and Henry's. But it was clear to me from that event that the two men had entered a new stage of life—as do all married couples—by stating their vows and love for each other in the company of those most important to them. And it wasn't just my imagination that things were different for Bill and Henry after their union ceremony. "Our parents treat us differently," said Bill. "There's no question now in their minds that we're a couple, and they don't hesitate to offer their advice, as they would to any married child and his spouse. Sometimes that's good, and sometimes that's not so good." Henry added, "The two of us also take the relationship even more seriously than we did before. It gives us a new sense of commitment and security. Having the ceremony was physically and emotionally exhausting, but I'm glad we did it."

Gay and lesbian couples have many different reasons for having commitment ceremonies, but most mirror those of heterosexual couples, whether the ceremony is an opportunity to formalize a commitment to each other or a plain and simple celebration of mutual love.

> **For gay and lesbian people in couple relationships,
> when you fill out a registration form at a doctor's
> office, for example, do you check the box for "married"
> or "single"?**

Some gay and lesbian people in couple relationships check "married," and some check "single." When faced with a form that offers only these two options, one lesbian friend writes in "lesbian couple," draws a box next to it, and checks it off.

> ### What happens when one partner in a couple gets sick?

When Jim's partner of two years, Paul, was diagnosed with AIDS, a few of his relatives asked Jim if he was going to stay with Paul or leave him. "I was floored," said Jim. "If my brother's wife had been diagnosed with breast cancer two years after they got married, they never would have asked him that question. How could they think I would abandon him?"

There are people, of course, heterosexual and homosexual, who abandon sick spouses, but those cases are by far the exception. More typical is the story of Paulene and Helen. Paulene was first diagnosed with breast cancer in the mid-1970s and has been through a succession of surgeries and rounds of chemotherapy and hormone therapy. Helen is as devoted to Paulene as anyone could possibly be, making certain she's taking her medication, accompanying her to treatments, and offering more love and support than anyone could hope for.

> ### Can a gay or lesbian spouse get medical benefits?

An ever-growing number of private companies, universities, and colleges, as well as government bodies, offer the same benefits— including medical insurance—to the spouses of gay and lesbian employees that they offer to heterosexual married couples. (For more information on this subject, see chapter 7, "Work.")

> ### What's it like when a heterosexual sibling gets married?

For many gay and lesbian people, a heterosexual sibling's marriage is often a reminder that no matter how comfortable they are being gay or lesbian, they are still different, and that no matter how accepting their parents are of their homosexuality, their couple relationship may not be celebrated with nearly as much enthusiasm as that of a heterosexual sibling.

Gay and lesbian people who haven't yet told their families they're gay can have an especially hard time. For Anita, her older sister's wedding meant having to answer the question, So when are you getting married? every two minutes for five hours. "But that wasn't the worst," said Anita. "When it came time to throw the bouquet, I hid in the bathroom. A search party came looking for me and dragged me back into the ballroom. My sister threw the bouquet right at me, so I had to catch it. What else could I do?"

Anita's family didn't know that her best friend, with whom she'd been sharing an apartment since graduating from college a couple of years earlier, was her romantic partner of three years. Anita added, "Somehow I doubt my parents will want to give me the same kind of wedding they gave my sister when they know the whole story. I can't imagine my family accepting me, let alone announcing to the whole world that their daughter is marrying another woman. Can you imagine the wedding invitations? It makes me so angry on so many levels, including the fact that I'll never have a full set of china!"

For gay and lesbian people who have told their families that they're gay, the wedding of a sibling can still cause all kinds of conflicts and mixed emotions. For example, when Ken's brother got married, the invitation to the wedding did not include Ted, Ken's partner of four years. "I was furious, but I didn't tell my brother how angry I was," said Ken. "I wasn't even sure at first if I was going to say anything. But Ted is my family, so I insisted that he be invited. But that wasn't the end of it. Then I had to figure out how to introduce Ted to my relatives, most of whom didn't know I was gay. I was sweating before we even got to the church."

> ### Do gay people marry heterosexual people? Why?

Many, many gay and lesbian people marry heterosexual people, and for a variety of reasons, including love.

Some gay and lesbian people marry heterosexuals because getting married is what we all learn is the right thing to do. Our culture is geared toward heterosexual married relationships, and some gay people, like heterosexual people, want to fit in and "do the right thing." Some of these men and women enter heterosexual marriages for cover, hoping to fulfill family or professional expectations. Some don't inform their opposite-gender spouses beforehand and some do, including plenty of closeted gay and lesbian celebrities over the years, who have made arrangements—financial and otherwise—with heterosexual opposite-gender partners.

Many gay men and lesbians at the time they marry an opposite-gender spouse are either in denial about their sexuality or simply not fully aware of their sexual feelings. When Katie married at the age of eighteen, she loved her husband, but she knew she "felt different from other girls," although she didn't know why. "It wasn't until I'd been married for seven years and had four children that I had my first adult crush on a woman. And would you believe it was a woman in the church choir? Even after Mary and I became sexually involved, it still took me another year to admit to myself that I was a lesbian. I couldn't even say the word!"

Some gay and lesbian people who marry partners of the opposite gender get married with the hope that they'll "get over" their homosexual feelings. That was exactly what Edward hoped when he married Suzanne. "We were both very young," said Edward, "and neither of us knew much of anything about homosexuality. I even told Suzanne that I had had these feelings, but the psychiatrist I was seeing reassured us I would get over it, and that the best thing I could do was get married and have children." Shortly after the birth of their second daughter, six years into their marriage, and after ten years of seeing the same psychiatrist, Edward left his wife. "I didn't get over it. In fact, by the time I left my wife—and fired my psychiatrist—I couldn't have been more certain that I was gay and that my psychiatrist was a quack."

> **How do heterosexual spouses react when they find out a spouse is gay?**

According to Amity Pierce Buxton, author of The Other Side of the Closet, a book about the coming-out crisis for heterosexual spouses of gay and lesbian people, heterosexual spouses greet the disclosure as a denial of the relationship. "Shocked spouses," she writes, "typically feel rejected sexually and bereft of the mates that they thought they had. . . . Although relieved to know the reason behind changes in their partner's behavior or problems in marital sex, most feel hurt, angry and helpless." And though their homosexual spouse most often feels relief in stepping out of the closet, and is likely to receive support from other gay and lesbian people, heterosexual spouses suddenly find themselves in a closet of their own, fearful of telling anyone the truth about their gay or lesbian spouse.

> **Do any of these marriages last after a spouse finds out?**

According to Buxton, "Although a number of couples succeed in preserving the marriage, the majority do not. Despite sincere efforts, the sexual disparity, competition for the partner's attention or unconventional—and for some, immoral—arrangements eventually become intolerable for most spouses."

> **What should you do if you think your spouse is lesbian or gay?**

Before you do anything, find help, preferably a counselor who has experience in dealing with your circumstances. Depending upon where you live, you may be able to find a support group for heterosexual people who have—or have had—gay or lesbian spouses. And you should also read Buxton's The Other Side of *the Closet,* which is listed in the bibliography at the back of this book.

> ### Do gay men and lesbians ever marry each other for "marriages of convenience"?

Yes, there are gay men and lesbians who have married each other and even had children together in order to appear heterosexual. Some people do it because of their careers—men and women in the military, for example—others to gain citizenship, and others, still, because of family pressures. I remember one young woman in college who came from a very prominent and wealthy family. From what she knew about her parents, she assumed that they would never let her take over the family business if they discovered she was a lesbian, so she set out to find and marry a gay man with a similar need to appear heterosexual.

I should also add that there are gay and lesbian people who are in denial about their sexual orientation, marry each other unknowingly, and discover during the course of their marriage that both are homosexual.

> ### Why do gay people hold hands in public?

Some gay people who hold hands in public do so to make a political statement, to make the point that gay people should be allowed to hold hands in public just as many heterosexual couples do without thinking twice. But most gay people who hold hands in public do so for the very same reasons that heterosexual people do: They simply want to hold the hand of someone they care about. But because of public hostility toward gay and lesbian people, particularly those who display any kind of affection in public for a same-gender partner, most gay people rarely hold hands in public without first considering where they are and whether holding hands would be a safe thing to do.

> **How do gay and lesbian couples split up?**

Gay and lesbian couples end their relationships in mostly the same ways married heterosexual couples do. It's just as painful, just as complex, and often just as ugly and messy. But there are differences. Because gay and lesbian people can't get legally married, they can't get legally divorced. This may sound appealing at first, because the partners can simply walk away from the relationship without even filing divorce papers. But without the legal protections that are built into marriage in the event of a divorce, dividing up property and arranging custody where children are involved can lead to a legal and emotional nightmare even greater than the messiest heterosexual divorce.

7

?

WORK

> **Are there professions that attract large numbers of gay people?**

Gay and lesbian people work in every profession, from the military to the arts, and do all kinds of jobs, from building roads to educating children. There are, however, certain professions and jobs that apparently attract a large number of gay or lesbian people. For example, it seems that a disproportionate number of male nurses, flight attendants, dancers, and figure skaters are gay. And it seems that a disproportionate number of female athletes, gym teachers, and military personnel—for example—are lesbians.

I've heard a number of possible explanations for this apparent phenomenon. I don't think any one explanation is adequate to explain why gay and lesbian people are represented in

greater numbers in some jobs and professions, but in the absence of any concrete answers, some of the explanations I've
heard are worth considering. One theory is that traditionally female professions attract gay men and traditionally male professions attract lesbians because gay men and lesbians are more
likely to feel comfortable about crossing gender lines. I don't
think I buy that theory. Another theory is that gay and lesbian
people are attracted to fields that have typically overlooked or
been accepting of homosexuality, like the arts.

One common stereotype is that gay men are attracted to
certain jobs because gay men are more likely than heterosexual men to be artistically gifted, and that lesbians are attracted
to certain jobs because lesbians are more likely than heterosexual women to be mechanically gifted. I think there's some
truth to this, but I don't have any studies to back me up.

Of the many explanations I've heard, I think it's easiest to
understand how the fear of discovery has led gay and lesbian
people to pursue certain jobs or professions and avoid others.
Journalist and writer Frank Browning noted: "In the past, once
you realized that you'd been sentenced to a homosexual life,
you assumed that a lot of worlds were closed to you because of
the social expectations. There are forms of social performance
that you're expected to meet, such as having a spouse and
bringing a spouse to social functions. For this reason, many
gay and lesbian people retreated into their own professional
worlds and became florists or dog groomers or whatever. They
pursued jobs and careers they could control, where they
wouldn't be subject to someone else's judgment." Browning
acknowledges that this is only a partial answer to a question
that still remains to be adequately addressed.

> ### Are gay people more likely to pursue artistic careers?

It appears that gay men, at least, are more likely to pursue artistic careers than are heterosexual men. The AIDS crisis made this

tragically clear during the 1980s through the mid-1990s with a disproportionately high number of deaths from AIDS among the ranks of male dancers, actors, figure skaters, musicians, designers, and other artistic professionals.

> *Are all male hairdressers, child-care workers, elementary schoolteachers, decorators, and dancers gay?*
> *Are all female professional athletes, gym teachers, and military personnel lesbians?*

No, but lots of gay men are hairdressers, child-care workers, elementary schoolteachers, decorators, and dancers. And lots of lesbians are professional athletes, gym teachers, and military personnel. Whether or not gay and lesbian people indeed fill a larger percentage of jobs in these professions as opposed to all other professions—as I strongly suspect they do—won't be known for certain until gay and lesbian people can be accurately surveyed. If it's found that gay and lesbian people do fill a larger percentage of these jobs, then we're still left with the "why" question.

I should add here that because gay and lesbian people work in every profession, you can't assume that all men who work in what we think of as typically male jobs, like truck drivers, are heterosexual. Similarly, not all women who work in what we think of as typically female jobs, like child-care workers, are heterosexual. And, of course, there are plenty of heterosexual male flight attendants, dancers, and florists, and plenty of heterosexual female gym teachers and athletes.

> *Should gay people be allowed to be teachers?*

Yes, and gay and lesbian teachers are already teaching in classrooms all across the country, as they have been for generations.

Those who object to gay and lesbian teachers in the classroom base their arguments on the mistaken twin assumptions that gay and lesbian teachers are more likely to molest their students than heterosexual teachers and that gay and lesbian teachers will set the wrong example and influence their students to become homosexuals.

First, the most likely person to molest children is a heterosexual male. His most likely victim is a female child. (For more on the subject of child molesting, see chapter 1, "The Basics," and the question "Are gay and lesbian people more likely to molest children?") Second, no one—not a teacher, a parent, or a favorite aunt—can influence anyone to "become" a homosexual. You can't "make" a homosexual. You are, or you aren't. The best a gay or lesbian teacher can do is be an inspiring educator and set an example as a positive role model to all children—to show them that someone can be a gay or lesbian person and a good teacher. Plenty of us, including this writer, would have welcomed some positive gay and lesbian role models as we struggled through school in isolation.

I like what a lesbian comedian once said about this point: "If teachers had that kind of influence over students, we'd all be nuns." The distinction here, of course, is that you can convince children to become nuns or priests. You cannot, however, convince anyone to become gay or lesbian.

> ### Should an openly gay teacher be allowed to teach?

This is an interesting distinction. Some people believe it's okay for gay and lesbian people to teach as long as they stay in the closet—in other words, hide the truth about who they are. It's okay as long as they leave their homosexuality at the front door.

Think for a second what it would mean for any teacher to leave his or her sexual orientation at the door. For a heterosexual teacher that would mean not wearing a wedding band to class, because the wedding band is a symbol of a heterosexual relationship. It would also mean that a heterosexual teacher could not bring a spouse to school social events. And it would also mean that if a student asked a personal question—for example, "Are you married?"—a married teacher would have to say, "I can't talk about my personal life," or would have to lie and say no.

Teachers are human, so inevitably their personal lives come up in class, particularly when students reach an age—junior high school, according to several teachers I spoke with—when they start asking teachers personal questions. Imagine what it's like for a gay or lesbian teacher when students ask, "Miss Shapiro, do you have a boyfriend?" "Are you married?" "How come we saw you on television in the Gay Pride march?" "Are you a lesbian?" A teacher who has to hide her homosexuality could not address any of these questions in an open and honest manner. And it goes beyond questions. "What am I supposed to do when students call each other 'fag' and 'dyke'?" said Miss Shapiro, who teaches at a large high school outside Denver. "Am I supposed to sit there and let them use words like that? Should I challenge them and tell them that saying 'fag' and 'dyke' is just as bad as saying 'nigger' and 'kike'? But then, because I'm defending gay people, my students might figure out that I'm a lesbian. And if they figure out I'm a lesbian, and someone complains to the administration, I could lose my job. Put yourself in my shoes. Would you want to live like that?"

> *Are there companies that specifically welcome gay people?*
> *Are there companies that provide benefits to gay couples?*

Yes. Increasingly, major corporations and smaller companies alike are making an effort to welcome gay and lesbian people by, for example, prohibiting discrimination on the basis of sexual orientation, offering domestic partner benefits, and organizing sensitivity training workshops.

Every year, GLV Ratings and Research conducts a survey of American companies and provides a list of the best 100 companies for gay and lesbian people to work for. Some of the companies on the 1998 list included Adolph Coors, America Online, American Express, Barnes & Noble, Bristol-Myers Squibb, Chevron, Foote Cone & Belding, General Mills, Intel, Inc., Lucent Technologies, Minnesota Mining and Manufacturing, Netscape, Pacific Bell, RJR Nabisco, Shell Oil, Starbucks, United Airlines, Volkswagen, Xerox, and Ziff Davis Publishing.

At a growing number of companies, gay and lesbian employees have organized their own employee groups. And due in large part to the research and lobbying efforts of these groups, more and more companies are considering extending or have already extended to the spouses of gay and lesbian employees many of the same benefits that are offered to married heterosexual spouses. Many small companies, as well as scores of major corporations, provide such benefits, including the New York Times, Microsoft, and Walt Disney. In addition, a growing number of cities, including New York, are providing domestic partner benefits to municipal employees and three states, New York, Vermont, and Oregon, provide such benefits to state employees.

Also, of course, gay and lesbian social service agencies and organizations, as well as businesses owned and run by gay men and lesbians, welcome gay and lesbian employees.

> ### What happens when gay and lesbian people come out at work or are found out?

Gay and lesbian people who come out of the closet at work or are found out have a range of experiences, from complete acceptance to being fired.

When Ralph was interviewing for his first job out of law school, he decided he didn't want his sexuality to become an issue after he was hired. So before he was made an offer at the firm where he had worked the previous summer, Ralph had a talk with the hiring partner. As he explained later: "If there was going to be a problem, I wanted to know in advance so I could look for a job elsewhere. I walked into the hiring partner's office and asked him if I could close the door. I told him I sensed there was a good chance they would offer me a job, and that they should know something about my personal life before they hired me—that I was gay. He asked me why I thought it was important to tell him that. I told him I didn't want it to come out later and then be a problem. He looked at me and said that that was exactly *his* problem. He was gay and had always kept it a secret." Ralph was offered the job, and he accepted it.

When Carolyn first interviewed for her job as a Christian educator in the heart of a low-income housing community in Atlanta, no one asked her about her sexuality. But three years after she was hired, she was called into her boss's office and told that a student who stayed in her home had come across some things that indicated she was a lesbian: "Their biggest accusation was that I wrote checks to a gay church and that this girl saw pictures of me in my photo album sitting on the hood of my car with my roommate, with my arms draped around her. My boss asked if I was a lesbian, and I said that he didn't have the right to ask me that. Then he said, 'If you can't tell us that you're not, we need your resignation.' I said, 'When do you want it?' It was clear to me that there was no changing his mind."

Not everyone is either accepted or fired. Billie, a schoolteacher in a city near San Francisco, knows she won't be fired if her principal finds out she's a lesbian, in part because her city forbids discrimination based on sexual orientation. "But I know they'll make my life so miserable that I'll have to quit," she said. "I hate living like this, but my partner is unemployed, and I can't afford to lose my job. So there's no way I would come out, and I'm doing everything I can to make sure no one finds out."

> **Why do people want to be openly gay at work?**

See chapter 3, "Coming Out."

> **Do some people have to stay in the closet at work?**

Yes. Any gay man or woman who serves in the military must remain in the closet or they'll be discharged. (See chapter 8, "The Military," for more on this subject.) There are also plenty of other people who could risk their jobs or count on being harassed by coworkers if they revealed their sexual orientation, particularly if they work for a company or a boss known to be unfriendly to gay people. And there are others still who fear that their careers would be hampered by public disclosure of their sexual orientation, including teachers, politicians, corporate executives, professional athletes, and high-profile actors and actresses.

> **Are there gay people who stay in the closet at work even though they don't have to?**

There are lots of people who choose to remain closeted even when there is little, if any, real risk that their careers would be jeopardized if it were known that they were gay. And this includes people who work for companies or live in places that specifically forbid discrimination against gay and lesbian people. These gay men and women choose to remain closeted for a couple of reasons. Some are simply accustomed to keeping their personal lives completely separate from their work lives. This includes many people who came of age at a time when being out on your job was unthinkable. Other people choose to remain in the closet because they fear the unknown. Will their colleagues be uncomfortable? What will their boss think? Will disclosure affect a promotion? These concerns can be especially acute when there are few—if any—colleagues who are openly gay. Not many people are willing to step into uncharted territory if that means potentially jeopardizing their livelihood.

> **Can you be fired from your job for being gay or
> lesbian?**

Absolutely. If you serve in the military and your homosexuality
becomes known, you will likely be discharged (see chapter 8,
"The Military"). And because federal civil rights legislation does
not include protection against discrimination in employment
based on sexual orientation, gay men and women can be fired
from their jobs unless such discrimination is expressly forbidden by their employer. Gay men and women are also protected
from discrimination in employment if they live in a state or mu-
nicipality that has passed legislation protecting gay men and
women from discrimination based on sexual orientation.

> **Are there places and companies where gay people are
> protected from discrimination, and can't be fired simply
> because of their sexual orientation?**

Fortunately, yes. Federal employees—other than those serving
in the military—are protected from discrimination, as are people who live in the ten states (California, Connecticut, Hawaii,
Massachusetts, Minnesota, New Hampshire, New Jersey,
Rhode Island, Vermont, and Wisconsin) and the scores of municipalities that have passed laws protecting gay and lesbian
people from discrimination based on sexual orientation. Also,
a growing number of smaller companies and seventy-five percent of the Fortune 500 companies, as well as many colleges
and universities have incorporated sexual orientation into
their nondiscrimination policies.

> **Can you be openly gay and succeed professionally?**

Not that long ago, almost all gay and lesbian people had to
hide their sexual orientation from their colleagues and employers for fear of being fired. But now there are more and

more examples of successful gay men and lesbians in a variety of professions who are open about who they are.

There are, however, exceptions, most visibly the military, where openly gay service members are rewarded with expulsion. Also, when it comes to professional sports, only a handful of athletes have chosen to come forward (see chapter 15, "Sports"). And while an increasing number of movie and television actors have come out about their homosexuality—notably Sir Ian McKellen, Ellen DeGeneres, Anne Heche, Dan Butler (from *Frasier*), and Amanda Bearse (*Married . . . with Children*)—most remain hidden. And at the highest levels of corporate America you'll have a hard time finding anyone who is openly gay or lesbian.

> **Aren't there famous people from the world of music who are openly gay?**

Indeed there are, and it doesn't seem to have hurt their careers one bit. They include Melissa Etheridge, k. d. lang, Boy George, Elton John, George Michael, and the Indigo Girls.

> **Do gay and lesbian people bring same-gender spouses or same-gender dates to office parties?**

Lots of gay and lesbian people wish they could bring their spouse or a same-gender date to company parties, but for several reasons very few do. To bring a same-gender spouse or date, you would have to be out of the closet at your job. To be out at your job, you would have to work at a company where gay and lesbian people are accepted. And even then, unless you worked for a company where there were other gay and lesbian employees who were comfortable bringing their partners, you would have to have enough courage and self-confidence to be one of the few same-gender couples (or the only one) at the party. Also, your same-gender spouse or date would have to be comfortable with the idea.

8

?

THE MILITARY

> **What is the U.S. government's policy on gay and lesbian people in the military?**

The official policy is known as "Don't Ask, Don't Tell, Don't Pursue," and it was the result of a 1993 compromise worked out between Congress, the Pentagon, and President Bill Clinton, following Clinton's ill-fated attempt to lift the U.S. military's complete ban on gay and lesbian people. Under this compromise policy, gay and lesbian people, as well as bisexuals, may serve in the military as long as they don't tell anyone about their sexual orientation and don't engage in homosexual acts (holding hands with someone of the same gender?). The military, for its part, is forbidden to question service members about their sexual orientation or investigate a service member without credible information that they have engaged in homosexual conduct.

The idea behind the new policy was that gay people, while being allowed to serve, would keep their orientation secret and remain celibate—thus preventing what the military claimed would result if openly gay people were allowed to serve: the destruction of morale and of unit cohesion.

Whatever the intent of the new policy, four years after "Don't Ask, Don't Tell, Don't Pursue" went into effect, the number of gay men and lesbians discharged from military service had increased by 67 percent.

> **What were the reasons the military gave in the first place for completely excluding gay men and lesbians from service?**

People in the military have over the years offered a long and changing list of reasons why gay and lesbian people shouldn't be permitted to serve in the military. Some of those who have opposed allowing gay people to serve once argued that gay men and lesbians were security risks because they could easily be blackmailed by someone threatening to reveal their secret life.

Retired General Colin Powell, who was the chairman of the Joint Chiefs of Staff at the time the new policy was worked out, and who strongly opposed lifting the ban against gay men and lesbians, stated on a number of occasions that "the presence of homosexuals in the force would be detrimental to good order and discipline, for a variety of reasons, principally relating around the issue of privacy." Others said that the presence of gay people would seriously impair the accomplishment of military missions by undermining discipline, morale, and cohesiveness among the troops. Still others have said that if homosexuals were allowed to openly declare their sexual orientation, heterosexuals who shower with gay men would have an "uncomfortable feeling of someone watching." (If servicemen are so fainthearted about the possibility of being looked at in the shower, the Pentagon should be worrying about how its soldiers will hold up on the battlefield.)

> ### How many gay people have been thrown out of the military?

Since 1943, when the military first began officially excluding homosexuals, between eighty thousand and one hundred thousand gay men and lesbians have been ousted from the military. According to the General Accounting Office, the annual cost of discharging and replacing homosexuals in the military is at least $27 million. And that figure does not take into account the human price—the thousands of ruined careers and lives.

> ### Do gay people make good soldiers?

Several reports, including three commissioned by the Pentagon itself, concluded that there was no evidence that homosexuals were any greater security risk than heterosexuals and that they were no more likely to be subject to blackmail. The reports also found no evidence that homosexuals disrupted the armed forces; in fact, they praised the performance of gay men and lesbians in the military, and urged their retention.

> ### What does the military do when it suspects that a soldier is lesbian or gay?

According to a New York Times report by Jennifer Egan, under the current policy, an inquiry cannot even begin "without credible information that a person has made a statement of homosexual orientation or engaged in homosexual conduct." Egan explains, however, that it's up to the commanding officer to decide what exactly constitutes "credible information." Inquiries are "often as simple as questioning the service member—or, in the practice, discouraged but still extant, known as witch hunting, pressing the service member for the names of other homosexuals in exchange for leniency." In one of the cases that Egan writes about, the inquiry included interviews with the service member's "parents, her childhood friends and even her prom dates—300 pages of testimony."

Once an inquiry is complete, Egan explains, "a commanding officer must decide whether a service member has, in fact, made a statement of homosexuality or engaged in homosexual acts, which the current policy defines as any bodily contact that 'a reasonable person' would understand to be for purposes of sexual gratification or an expression of homosexuality—in some cases, as little as a kiss, a hug or handholding. If the C.O. determines that a basis for discharge exists, he or she will initiate 'separation' proceedings—the administrative process whereby a service member may be prematurely discharged."

The late Randy Shilts, who documented the experiences of gay people in the military in his 1993 book, *Conduct Unbecoming: Gays and Lesbians in the U.S. Military*, found examples of gay men and women under investigation who were threatened with jail terms, as well as dishonorable discharges and the loss of military benefits, unless they turned over the names of other gay men and lesbians.

> **Is there an organization that helps gay people who are facing discharge from the military?**

SLDN, the Servicemembers Legal Defense Network, is "the sole national legal aid and watchdog organization that assists servicemembers hurt by the Don't Ask, Don't Tell, Don't Pursue policy." (For contact information see, "Resources.")

> **Why do gay people want to be in the military?**

In today's all-volunteer military, gay and lesbian people join for all the same reasons that heterosexual people do: pay, training, educational benefits, camaraderie, overseas travel, leadership challenges, and often a patriotic desire to serve their country. Some gay and lesbian people in the military also say they want to prove that gay people can serve in the Marine Corps, for example, and still be successful.

> **Why do gay people join the military knowing they could be discharged if they're found out?**

Many of the gay and lesbian people currently in the military joined at a time in their lives when they were still either uncertain about their sexual orientation or in deep denial about their homosexual feelings. Others knew they were gay or lesbian but saw the same career opportunities, or had the same desire to serve, as their heterosexual counterparts and gambled that they could keep their sexual orientation a secret.

> **When did gay people first begin challenging the military's antigay policies?**

Gay rights activists first challenged the U.S. military's ban on gay and lesbian people in 1964, when a handful of protesters picketed the Whitehall Induction Center in New York City, demanding that homosexuals be allowed to enlist. In 1975, Sergeant Leonard Matlovich and Ensign Copy Berg, both of whom were being discharged because they were gay, brought the first two lawsuits against the military in a bid to retain their jobs and overturn the military's antigay policy.

> **How have gay people managed to stay in the military?**

Most gay and lesbian people have managed to stay in the military by carefully guarding their secret, often constructing a heterosexual life as cover. For some gay and lesbian people this has included marrying a person of the opposite gender to give the appearance of being in a heterosexual marriage. Other gay and lesbian people have simply pretended to be heterosexual, laughed at jokes about gay people, and told stories about fictional heterosexual escapades when they had to.

Not all gay and lesbian people in the military have remained completely in the closet. Some have been known as gay or lesbian to their colleagues and superior officers and have been protected by them.

❭ How do other countries handle the issue of gay people in the military?

With the exception of Great Britain, most European countries, as well as Israel, permit openly gay and lesbian people to serve in the military. Canada lifted its ban against gay men and women in October 1992, after a court ruled that its policy of exclusion violated the 1982 Canadian Charter of Rights and Freedom. The Royal New Zealand Navy is actively working to make itself a welcoming place for gay and lesbian people, encouraging "a climate where those who choose to declare their sexual orientation can do so without risking retaliation."

9

?

WHERE GAY AND LESBIAN PEOPLE LIVE

> *Where do gay and lesbian people live?*

From watching television news reports, you might think that gay
and lesbian people live only in New York, San Francisco, and Los
Angeles. Not true. Gay and lesbian people live everywhere, from
rural Kentucky to downtown Juneau, Alaska. It is true, however,
that large numbers of gay and lesbian people migrate from rural
areas and small towns and cities to large metropolitan areas.

> *Why do gay and lesbian people move from smaller towns
> and cities to places like San Francisco and New York?*

Large cities have for many decades been magnets for gay and
lesbian people in search of other people like themselves. San

Francisco, New York, Chicago, Los Angeles, and the nation's other major cities have long had significant gay and lesbian subcultures, including gay bars and restaurants. More recently, these cities have also developed significant gay and lesbian communities, complete with community centers, softball teams, choruses, and countless social, religious, and professional organizations. Also, large cities have traditionally provided the kind of anonymity that has allowed gay and lesbian people to keep their homosexual identities safely hidden, particularly from their families back home.

Although the major cities have long been popular with gay and lesbian people, it was World War II, according to historians John D'Emilio and Allan Bérubé, that led to the explosion of urban gay and lesbian subcultures. They explain that tens of millions of American men and women were uprooted during the war to serve in the military and to work in the war industries. Most of these men and women, including millions of gay and lesbian young people, moved to or traveled through the major industrial and port cities. It was in New York, Chicago, Los Angeles, San Francisco, and other cities that these gay and lesbian people discovered for the first time that they weren't alone.

Following the war, rather than return to the small cities and towns they once called home, many gay and lesbian people chose to remain in the major cities.

> ### How did San Francisco become such a popular place with gay and lesbian people?

One possible explanation for San Francisco's popularity among gay and lesbian people early on, besides its status as a major port city and its long-standing reputation for tolerating people who lead unconventional lives, was suggested to me by San Francisco Municipal Court Judge Herbert Donaldson.

As a young attorney, Donaldson was involved with an early gay rights organization in San Francisco called the Society for Individual Rights. SIR, along with other gay and lesbian organizations in San Francisco, planned a fund-raising ball for the evening of January 1, 1965. The event turned into a major confrontation between the police, who didn't want the event to take place, and the hundreds of gay and lesbian people who attended. Several people were arrested, including Donaldson.

According to Donaldson, "The police made this estimate that there were seventy thousand homosexuals in the city. There weren't, but when they carry it on the [news] wire services that there are seventy thousand, you've got seventy thousand others out in the country who want to come and join that seventy thousand here! They're still coming."

By the 1970s, San Francisco's large and politically active gay and lesbian population, in combination with the city's reputation as a relatively friendly place for gay men and lesbians and its mild climate and physical beauty, had made it a popular destination for gay people in search of a better life.

> ### Why do gay and lesbian people create their own neighborhoods in the major cities?

Some—not most—gay and lesbian people live in predominantly gay neighborhoods, and they do so for many of the same reasons people from different ethnic, racial, and religious groups often wind up segregated into their own neighborhoods: safety, comfort, community, a sense of feeling welcome, and discrimination.

It's no secret that gay and lesbian people are often targets of physical attacks. Living in a predominantly gay neighborhood offers the safety of knowing that your neighbor is unlikely to attack you for being gay. Unfortunately, these neighborhoods are also often destinations for people looking for a gay person to attack.

Living in a community where there are lots of other gay and lesbian people or where gay and lesbian people make up the majority of residents is for many men and women more comfortable than living where they're the only gay people or gay couple in the neighborhood. For single men and women, a predominantly gay and lesbian neighborhood also offers more opportunities to meet and socialize with other gay and lesbian people.

In San Francisco's Castro neighborhood, many of the shopkeepers, as well as the doctors, dentists, tailors, and so forth, are gay or lesbian, or gay-friendly, so you can be yourself and not worry about being judged. You also don't have to worry about discrimination. For example, if you're looking for an apartment with your same-gender partner in a predominantly gay neighborhood, you aren't likely to encounter a landlord who doesn't rent to gay people or to gay and lesbian couples.

> *What are some gay neighborhoods, and what are they like?*

Most major cities have neighborhoods that are popular with gay and lesbian people. For example, in Washington, D.C., it's the Dupont Circle neighborhood, which is popular as well with young nongay families and single people. In Los Angeles, it's West Hollywood, which is actually an incorporated city. In New York City, it's Chelsea and Greenwich Village. And in Houston, it's the Montrose neighborhood.

Most city neighborhoods popular with gay and lesbian people look very much like any other neighborhood except that there are stores, restaurants, and bars that cater to a gay and lesbian clientele. You also might see more identifiably gay and lesbian people on the street. And occasionally you'll see same-gender couples holding hands.

The first time I walked down Castro Street, the main commercial street of San Francisco's predominantly gay and lesbian neighborhood, I was a little uncomfortable. Even though I'm gay, I had never been on a public street where there were so many gay and lesbian people. That may sound funny, but it wasn't something I was used to. This was just before Gay Pride Day in 1980, so Castro Street was overflowing with gay and lesbian tourists.

For me, the most startling sight was the many same-gender couples holding hands. People were behaving so normally—in other words, not censoring their behavior for heterosexual public consumption—that at first it didn't seem normal to me. Years later, I'm still surprised to see two people of the same gender holding hands on the street, but rather than think of it as abnormal, I'm now struck by the courage it takes to act normally in a world that is often so dangerous for people publicly identifiable as gay or lesbian.

> **What is it like for gay people who live outside the major cities—in the suburbs, for example?**

Gay men and lesbians, no matter where they live, have had all kinds of experiences, both positive and negative, with their heterosexual neighbors. For Connie and Renata, who decided to move from New York City to a suburban, almost rural, neighborhood in New Jersey, the experience was mixed. The two women, who had been a couple for nearly twenty years, didn't anticipate problems with their new neighbors, but they were a little apprehensive. "We thought we might have some problems, but we had our hopes up," said Connie.

One afternoon, a few months after they moved in, Connie and Renata found the word *dyke* spray-painted on their front door. "That scared us to death," said Renata, "but we decided to repaint the door and hope that it wouldn't happen again." It didn't—in part, they think, because they made a concerted effort to get to know their neighbors. "We hoped that once people got to know us, they'd treat us just like any other neighbors," said Connie.

Do they have any regrets? "No. This was something we wanted to do," said Renata. "We weren't twenty-five anymore, so we didn't care about nightlife. We just wanted peace and quiet and a backyard. That sounds hopelessly dull, but it's what we wanted. Maybe we should have done a better job of anticipating that not everyone would welcome us, but we've learned—and our neighbors have learned—from the experience."

SOCIALIZING AND FRIENDS

> *Where do gay people meet?*

Gay and lesbian people meet in all the places heterosexual people meet, from the grocery store, the office, and singles bars to professional organizations, social clubs, and on the Internet. But unless the singles bar, professional organization, or on-line chat room is specifically for gay and lesbian people, gay people must assume that almost everyone they meet is not gay.

> *Why do gay and lesbian people go to bars and belong to organizations that are just for gay people?*

When you're gay or lesbian, you are by definition an outsider: outside the norm, outside the mainstream, different. And no matter how well integrated you are into your community, college, profession, or family, you are still not a part of the majority.

When you enter a gay or lesbian bar or play on an all-gay softball team, you're no longer an outsider—you're normal. You can be yourself, which includes being physically affectionate in a way that heterosexual people take for granted. There's no fear of being judged or discriminated against for being gay. At its best, the experience offers the sense of being with "family."

When I attended the first conference of the National Lesbian and Gay Journalists Association in San Francisco, the experience was extraordinary. More than three hundred gay and lesbian journalists attended, and while there was plenty of disagreement about all kinds of political and professional issues, it was great to share experiences and ideas with gay and lesbian journalists from across the country and the professional spectrum. For many who attended, the conference was their first opportunity to talk with other gay and lesbian journalists.

I hasten to add that gay and lesbian people aren't one big happy family. Gay people are just as capable as anyone else of making all kinds of judgments, whether about race, age, looks, or the way you dress. For example, Craig, who is in his mid-twenties, thought he would feel welcome when he began socializing in the gay world. "What I quickly discovered," he said, "was that I was incredibly naive. When I walked into a bar— and that's assuming I could get in without having to show three types of identification—the first thing people saw was a black man, not just another gay man. You can't believe the stereotypes people hold on to. If I meet one more white man who thinks I'm some sort of sexual amazon just because I'm black, I'll scream. I thought gay people would know better—and some do—but more often than not, gay people and straight people treat me just the same."

› *What is a gay bar like?*

First, it's important to understand that gay and lesbian bars have historically played a key role in gay and lesbian social life because until fairly recently, bars were the only public places gay people could meet and socialize. Though that's often no longer the case, particularly in major cities, bars still play an important role as a gathering place for gay men and women.

There are all kinds of gay and lesbian bars. In big cities like New York, Chicago, and Los Angeles, different bars cater to different kinds of people. There are bars for men, women, older men, younger men; there are country and western bars, young professional bars, hustler bars, bars with back rooms (for those interested in sexual encounters), S&M bars—you name it. In smaller cities and towns, there may be only one bar for everyone. On a visit to Juneau, Alaska, several years ago, I went to what was then that city's one gay and lesbian bar. It was at the back of a restaurant a few blocks from downtown. The bar itself was about six feet in length. There were eight stools and enough room for another four people to stand. You had to meet everyone in the bar, because there was no way not to. The bartender joked that the bar was gay only until someone heterosexual walked in.

The first time I went to a gay bar, I was seventeen and very scared. I don't know what I thought went on in a bar, but to me the whole thing was mysterious, even exotic, but nonetheless terrifying. My friend Bob, who was my tour guide, told me what to expect, that it would be no different from a nongay singles bar, except that there would be no women. I was too embarrassed to tell Bob I had never been to any singles bar.

We walked through the door; no one checked my ID, even though I was underage. The place was dimly lit, smoky, and very crowded. The music was too loud for real conversation, but people were talking. On the left, men were seated at the bar. Men were also standing along the walls and talking in groups. Most were casually dressed in jeans and pressed shirts. The average age was probably thirty. Lots of people were just standing around looking at each other and looking a little bored. We stayed for about half an hour and left.

❯ What kinds of social organizations do gay people have?

Gay and lesbian people have all kind of organizations, from gay and lesbian college fraternities and alumnae and alumni groups to square dancing and gardening clubs, computer user groups, and marching bands. A recent events calendar for New York City's Lesbian & Gay Community Services Center listed 168 different predominantly gay and lesbian organizations (or organizations that hold meetings specifically for gay and lesbian people). Here's a sampling: ACT UP (AIDS Coalition to Unleash Power), African Ancestral Lesbians United for Social Change, Asians and Friends of New York, Axios Eastern and Orthodox Christians, BiGLTYNY (Bisexual, Gay, Lesbian, Transgender Youth of New York), Bisexual S/M Discussion Group, Bisexual Women's Group, Body Positive (support group of HIV-positive people), Broadway Night Out Theatre Spotlight, Butch/Femme Society, Christian Gays & Lesbians, Christian Science Group, Clann An Uabhair (Gay Scottish Society), Date Bait, Dignity/Big Apple (social events and liturgies for gay and lesbian Catholics), Empire State Pride Agenda, Fire-FLAG (Fire Fighters Lesbian and Gay of New York), Gay and Lesbian Alliance Against Defamation, Gay and Lesbian Arabs, Gay and Lesbian Independent Democrats, Gay and Lesbian Reading Group, Gay and Lesbian Sierrans, Gay Asian and Pacific Islander Men of New York, Gay Male S/M Activists, Gay Men of African Descent, Gay Men's

Opera Club, Gay Officers Action League, Gay Pilots Association, Girth and Mirth Club of New York, Heritage of Pride (organizers of New York City's Gay Pride events), Irish Lesbian and Gay Organization, Japanese Speaking Lesbigay Society, Knights Wrestling Club, Las Buenas Amigas Lesbianas Latinas en Nueva York, Latino Gay Men of New York, Lesbian and Gay People of Color Steering Committee, Lesbian and Gay Teachers Association, Lesbian Breast Cancer Support Group, Log Cabin Club, Manhattan Mustangs (country and western dance social club), Married Lesbians, Men of All Colors Together, Metro Gay Wrestling Alliance, Metropolitan Community Church, National Lesbian & Gay Journalists Association, Natural History Group, New York Advertising and Communications Network, New York Bankers Group, New York CyberQueers, Organization of Lesbian and Gay Architects and Designers, Prime Timers, Professionals in Film/Video, Psychology Discussion Group, Puerto Rican Initiative to Develop Empowerment, Scrabblers, Sirens Motorcycle Club, South Asian Lesbian and Gay Association, Spanish Language Club, Stonewall Democratic Club, Sundance Outdoor Adventure Society, Times Squares (square dance club), Transgender Rights, Twenty-Something, Village Dive Club, Village Playwrights, Women Drawing Women . . . And this list doesn't include the Gay Men's Chorus, and Front Runners, and . . .

> ### What do gay and lesbian people talk about when they get together?

In addition to talking about all the things that heterosexual people talk about, many gay and lesbian people talk about being gay and about the latest news on gay and lesbian rights issues.

An acquaintance once asked me why gay people make such a big deal about being gay and talk about it all the time. I explained that once being gay is no longer a big deal within our society, and once our civil rights are no longer questioned, we will probably stop talking about it.

> **Why are there so many gay people in Provincetown?**

Provincetown, on Cape Cod, is one of several resort areas popular with gay and lesbian people. Others include Palm Springs, California; Rehoboth Beach, Delaware; the Pines and Cherry Grove on Fire Island in New York; and Key West, Florida. These resorts offer hotels, restaurants, stores, and bars that cater to gay and lesbian people. Beyond the physical amenities, these resorts offer something no other resorts can offer gay people: lots of other gay and lesbian people. When you travel to one of these resort areas, you don't have to worry about being the only gay or lesbian person on the street or at the beach.

Of all these resorts, the Pines and Cherry Grove on Fire Island offer the "gayest" environment. Accessible only by ferry from the eastern end of Long Island, these two small summer communities are almost entirely populated by gay and lesbian people, which means you can feel entirely safe holding your sweetheart's hand in public and not draw a single stare.

> **Do lesbians and gay men get along?**

Historically, within the gay and lesbian rights movement, there have been tensions between lesbians and gay men, and often for good reason. In the early days, back in the 1950s, most gay men treated lesbians the way most heterosexual men treated women. "They thought we were there to serve coffee and doughnuts," said one activist, now in her seventies. But though there have always been tensions and often distance between the gay male and lesbian worlds, and despite the fact that plenty of lesbians have nothing to do with gay men and plenty of gay men have nothing to do with lesbians, there have also been many long-lasting friendships between lesbians and gay men. In addition, the AIDS crisis led to many close ties between gay men and lesbians, as they worked side by side caring for ill friends, and in AIDS professional and volunteer organizations.

> **Do gay and lesbian people have heterosexual friends?**

Most gay and lesbian people have nongay friends, and depending on the friendship, some gay and lesbian people choose to come out to their heterosexual friends and others don't. This isn't to say that those who don't come out are necessarily hiding anything from their heterosexual friends. The fact that they're gay may be self-evident, especially if they have a same-gender partner; they simply may choose not to talk about it. Other gay men and lesbians feel perfectly comfortable discussing their sexual orientation with heterosexual friends, whether it's in the context of relationship issues or politics.

Some gay and lesbian people choose not to have heterosexual friends. They may feel uncomfortable around nongay people or may simply prefer the companionship of other gay men and lesbians.

> **Do gay people lose nongay friends when they come out of the closet?**

It depends on the friends. Often friends can handle the news, but sometimes they can't. Nancy came out to her friends when she was in college. Most of her friends were supportive, but when Nancy told her best friend, "she got real distant. It's upsetting, and it still upsets me because we had been such good friends. It was such a catch-22 kind of thing, because I needed my friends most at that time, but I also feared my friends because I didn't know how they would react if they knew I was gay."

> *Why do some heterosexual women have a lot of gay*
> *male friends? Isn't there a nickname for such women?*

The phenomenon of friendships between gay men and heterosexual women has been the subject of newspaper and magazine articles, books, films (including *The Object of My Affection* and
My Best Friend's Wedding), and, in the fall of 1998, a television
show called *Will & Grace*. I'll leave the psychological analysis to
the mental health professionals, but I think my friend Sally offered the simplest explanation based on her own experience.
She said, "Many straight men are pigs. Seriously, I don't want
to say anything that knocks straight men, but do you think I'll
ever meet a straight man who likes the arts and gardening?
Those are the things I talk to my gay friends about. Also, I find
that my gay men friends have done a lot of soul-searching and
self-examination, and that's made them empathetic people.
And I know I can talk to them about life issues that involve not
following the crowd. They're supportive of me and the risks
I've taken with my life and work. And in general they're more
understanding than my women friends. Women care about
men. My gay friends care about me."

Women who have lots of gay male friends are sometimes
called "fag hags." While I know there are people who consider
this an endearing term, I generally find it offensive, as do
many women.

> *If you think a friend is gay, what should you say?*

If you're perfectly happy with your friendship, you don't have
to say anything. But if you feel that there is tension or distance
in your friendship and that the likely reason is your friend's
hidden homosexuality, then you may want to bring it up. You
can do this by speaking to your friend or writing your friend a
note.

Some people have no difficulty asking a friend directly, "Are you gay?" or telling a friend: "You're my friend, I care about you. I have the feeling that you're gay or lesbian and I want you to know that if this is the case I'm perfectly comfortable with that and completely supportive."

Not everyone likes to take the direct approach, so you may choose to let your friend know that you're familiar with and supportive of gay people by mentioning something you saw on television that was sympathetic to gay people or that you read something in the news about antigay violence or prejudice that upset you. This gives your friend an opening if he or she chooses to come out to you.

Keep in mind that many gay and lesbian people assume that if their nongay friends don't raise the subject, those friends either don't know or don't want to hear about their friend's homosexuality. If the letters I receive from concerned heterosexual men and women about their gay friends is any clue, there are a lot of nongay men and women out there waiting for their gay friends to say something. In general they haven't broached the subject with their gay and lesbian friends because they assume it's something their gay friends don't want to talk about or find embarrassing. The result is that everyone is so afraid to risk bringing it up that no one says anything and everyone winds up feeling uncomfortable.

My suggestion to gay and lesbian people and to nongay people who have gay and lesbian friends is this: If you want to come out to your nongay friends, don't wait for them to bring it up; and if you want to tell your gay and lesbian friends that you know they're gay and that it's not an issue for you, don't wait for them to bring it up. In either case, fight your fear and do it.

‖

?

RELIGION

> **Is homosexuality a sin?**
> **Is homosexuality immoral?**

No, homosexuality is not a sin and it is not immoral. Of course, not everyone will agree with me, but fortunately, we live in a nation where morality and religious beliefs are not legislated but are a matter of personal choice.

In recent years, these questions of whether or not homosexuality is immoral or sinful have been the subject of great debate. The result has been enormous conflict within the nation's mainstream religions and continuing heated discussion within American society. The following thoughts are from just three of the many people who have offered definitive progay responses to the questions of morality and sin.

Frank Kameny, who was fired from his job at the U.S. Army Map Service in 1957 because he was gay, first examined the morality question as part of his fight to get his job back. Kameny pursued his case right up to the U.S. Supreme Court, and in preparing his petition to the Supreme Court in late 1960, he concluded that homosexuality was moral. "At that time, the government put its disqualification of gays under the rubric of immoral conduct, which I objected to," Kameny explained. "Because under our system, morality is a matter of personal opinion and individual belief on which any American citizen may hold any view he wishes and upon which the government has no power or authority to have any view at all. Besides which, in my view, homosexuality is not only not immoral, but is affirmatively moral. Up until that time nobody else ever said this—as far as I know—in any kind of a formal court pleading." The Supreme Court refused to hear Kameny's case, and he later went on to form a pioneering gay rights organization in Washington, D.C. In part because of Kameny's dogged efforts, the federal government officially stopped excluding homosexuals from government employment in 1975.

Carolyn Mobley, an assistant pastor for the Metropolitan Community Church, a Christian church whose membership is primarily gay and lesbian, at first believed that her sexual orientation was sinful. But then as a college student she realized that her sexuality was not sinful but, instead, a gift from God. She credited the Rev. Martin Luther King, Jr., with helping her come to terms with being a lesbian: "Dr. King's commitment to disobeying unjust laws had a profound impact on my thinking. I began to question the things that I was told to do. Are they really right? Are they right if I'm told they're right by a person in a position of authority? I began to realize that parents could steer you wrong. Teachers could steer you wrong. Preachers, God knows, could steer you wrong. They were all fallible human beings. That really changed my way of looking at myself and the world. And it certainly helped me reevaluate the message I was getting from the church about homosexuality. It made me examine more closely what Scripture had to say about it.

"I continuously read Scripture on my own. I especially reread Romans numerous times. I finally got the picture that God wasn't against homosexuals. And that even Paul, who wrote that passage in Romans about homosexuality and was against homosexuals, was a human being subject to error, just like me. So I thought the man was wrong, period. What he was espousing was inaccurate, and it needed to be challenged. That was what Dr. King was about, challenging error wherever it was found.

"I continued to reinterpret that whole Romans scripture about giving up what was natural for something unnatural, and a light went off in my head. Paul had a point. His argument about doing what was natural really did make sense, but you had to know what was natural for you. It was unnatural for me to have sex with a man, so I decided that I wouldn't do that again. The only natural thing was for me to do what I'd been feeling since day one in the world. Why would I try to change that? How foolish I'd been. I thought to myself, Thank you, Paul. I got your message, brother. We're okay.

"When that light went on in my head, I knew it was from God, that it was my deliverance. God didn't deliver me from my sexuality. God delivered me from guilt and shame and gave me a sense of pride and wholeness that I really needed. My sexuality was a gift from God, and so is everyone's sexuality, no matter how it's oriented. It's a gift to be able to love."

Episcopal Bishop John Shelby Spong, an outspoken supporter of the ordination of gay and lesbian people and the blessing of same-gender relationships, also believes that homosexuality is not a sin. When asked by Parents, Friends, and Families of Lesbians and Gays whether, in his opinion, God regards homosexuality as a sin, he answered: "Some argue that since homosexual behavior is 'unnatural,' it is contrary to the order of creation. Behind this pronouncement are stereotypic definitions of masculinity and femininity that reflect the rigid gender categories of patriarchal society. There is nothing unnatural about any shared love, even between two of the same gender, if that experience calls both partners into a fuller state of being. Contemporary research is uncovering new facts that are producing rising conviction that homosexuality, far from being a sickness, sin, perversion, or unnatural act, is a healthy, natural, and affirming form of human sexuality for some people. Findings indicate that homosexuality is a given fact in the nature of a significant portion of people, and that it is unchangeable.

"Our prejudice rejects people or things outside our understanding. But the God of creation speaks and declares, 'I have looked out on everything I have made and "behold it [is] very good"' (Genesis 1:31). The word of God in Christ says that we are loved, valued, redeemed, and counted as precious no matter how we might be valued by a prejudiced world."

> ### What does the Bible say about gay men and lesbians?

The Bible doesn't say anything about same-gender sexual orientation as we understand it today. The Bible does, however, discuss same-gender sexual relations, but in fact doesn't say all that much about sex between men and says absolutely nothing about sex between women. Among the Bible's 31,173 verses, there are fewer than a dozen verses that mention sexual acts between men.

I like what Peter J. Gomes, an American Baptist minister and professor of Christian morals at Harvard, had to say in a *New York*

Times editorial regarding what is written in the Bible about homosexuality: "Christians opposed to political and social equality for homosexuals nearly always appeal to the moral injunctions of the Bible, claiming that Scripture is very clear on the matter and citing verses that support their opinion. They accuse others of perverting and distorting texts contrary to their 'clear' meaning. They do not, however, necessarily see quite as clear a meaning in biblical passages on economic conduct, the burdens of wealth, and the sin of greed.

"Nine biblical citations are customarily invoked as relating to homosexuality. Four (Deuteronomy 23:17, 1 Kings 14:24, 1 Kings 22:46, and 2 Kings 23:7) simply forbid prostitution by men and women. Two others (Leviticus 18:19–23 and Leviticus 20:10–16) are part of what biblical scholars call the Holiness Code. The code explicitly bans homosexual acts. But it also prohibits eating raw meat, planting two different kinds of seed in the same field and wearing garments with two different kinds of yarn. Tattoos, adultery, and sexual intercourse during a woman's menstrual period are similarly outlawed.

"There is no mention of homosexuality in the four Gospels of the New Testament. The moral teachings of Jesus are not concerned with the subject.

"Three references from St. Paul are frequently cited (Romans 1:26–2:1, 1 Corinthians 6:9–11, and 1 Timothy 1:10). But St. Paul was concerned with homosexuality only because in Greco-Roman culture it represented a secular sensuality that was contrary to his Jewish-Christian spiritual idealism. He was against lust and sensuality in anyone, including heterosexuals. To say that homosexuality is bad because homosexuals are tempted to do morally doubtful things is to say that heterosexuality is bad because heterosexuals are likewise tempted. For St. Paul, anyone who puts his or her interest ahead of God's is condemned, a verdict that falls equally upon everyone.

"And lest we forget Sodom and Gomorrah, recall that the story is not about sexual perversion and homosexual practice. It is about inhospitality, according to Luke 10:10–13, and failure to take care of the poor, according to Ezekiel 16:49–50: 'Behold, this was the iniquity of thy sister Sodom, pride, fullness of bread, and abundance of idleness was in her and in her daughters, neither did she strengthen the hand of the poor and needy.' To suggest that Sodom and Gomorrah is about homosexual sex is an analysis of about as much worth as suggesting that the story of Jonah and the whale is a treatise on fishing."

Gomes goes on to say later in his editorial that "those who speak for the religious right do not speak for all American Christians, and the Bible is not theirs alone to interpret. The same Bible that the advocates of slavery used to protect their wicked self-interests is the Bible that inspired slaves to revolt and their liberators to action.

"The same Bible that the predecessors of [the Rev. Jerry] Falwell and [the Rev. Pat] Robertson used to keep white churches white is the source of the inspiration of the Rev. Martin Luther King, Jr., and the social reformation of the 1960s.

"The same Bible that antifeminists use to keep women silent in the churches is the Bible that preaches liberation to captives and says that in Christ there is neither male nor female, slave nor free.

"And the same Bible that on the basis of an archaic social code of ancient Israel and a tortured reading of Paul is used to condemn all homosexuals and homosexual behavior includes metaphors of redemption, renewal, inclusion and love—principles that invite homosexuals to accept their freedom and responsibility in Christ and demand that their fellow Christians accept them as well."

> **What did Jesus have to say about homosexuals or homosexuality?**

Nothing.

> **What do different religions say about gay men and lesbians?**

The only thing the many different religions agree on about homosexuality is that they don't agree. That goes for different religions as well as different denominations within religions and different religious leaders within the same denomination. But for the sake of bringing a little order to the cacophony of discordant voices within the religious world, here's a general survey of what the major religions in the United States have to say on the subject, drawn, in part, from the *San Francisco Examiner*.

The United Methodists let openly gay people join and do not officially consider homosexuality a sin, but the United Methodists do consider homosexual activity "incompatible with Christian teaching." Nonetheless, more than 140 "reconciling congregations" have declared themselves to publicly welcome the full participation of gay men and lesbians, and a group of Methodist ministers has declared that they will perform same-gender unions.

The Mormon Church does not let openly gay people join, considers homosexuality a sin, and recommends chastity for homosexuals.

The Roman Catholic Church permits openly gay people to join, considers homosexuality morally wrong and a sin if practiced, and teaches that any sexual activity outside marriage is wrong. But Roman Catholic bishops in the United States issued a pastoral letter in 1997 advising parents of gay children to love and support their sons and daughters. In their letter the bishops said that homosexual orientation is not freely chosen and that parents must not reject their gay children in a society full of rejection and discrimination. The letter, which goes on to state that sexual activity between same-gender partners is immoral, urges parents to encourage their children to lead a chaste life. And just in case anyone thought otherwise, the bishops noted that the letter should not be understood "as an endorsement of what some would call 'a homosexual life style.'"

The Baptists officially let openly gay people join and consider homosexuality a sin, but the American Baptists and Southern Baptists differ in their views, and individual churches are autonomous. So although the Southern Baptist Convention may condemn homosexuality as "a manifestation of a depraved nature" and "a perversion of divine standards," one of its member churches, the Pullen Memorial Baptist Church in Raleigh, North Carolina, held a "blessing of holy union" for two gay men. That church was later ousted from the national convention, and the Southern Baptists subsequently amended their constitution to make clear that "homosexual behavior" was not to be approved or endorsed by any affiliated church.

The Episcopal Church lets openly gay people join, does not consider homosexuality a sin, and urges congregations to provide dialogues on human sexuality. But the Episcopal Church, which is one of the thirty-seven church provinces within the global Anglican Communion, was rocked by a resolution passed at the once-a-decade Lambeth Conference in 1998. The nearly eight hundred bishops who attended from around the world voted to reject homosexual practice as "incompatible with Scripture." That resolution led New York's Episcopal bishop and his eventual successor to write a joint letter to the sixty-two thousand Episcopalians in their flock reassuring them that "the character of our life together" as New York Episcopalians would remain the same. "This diocese," they wrote, "has long recognized and treasured the ministry of gay and lesbian Episcopalians in New York, and of course, the ministry of our gay and lesbian clergy."

The Lutherans let openly gay people join, consider homosexuality a sin, and believe that it is not in God's original plan. Presbyterians don't have one voice on this issue except regarding the ordination of gay and lesbian people: The highest court of the Presbyterian Church ruled in November 1992 that an openly gay, sexually active person cannot serve as a minister of any of its 11,500 churches; the ruling nullified the hiring of a gay woman as a copastor of a church in Rochester, New York.

Moslems do not let openly gay people join, consider homosexuality one of the worst sins, and encourage homosexuals to change. Orthodox Jews believe that homosexuality is an abomination, but on the other end of the Jewish spectrum, the Reform and Reconstructionist movements have established special outreach programs for gay and lesbian people and have even accepted them publicly into their rabbinical associations. Covering the middle ground of Judaism is the Conservative movement, which has welcomed gay and lesbian people to its congregations but does not allow them to become rabbis.

The best news comes from the Unitarian Universalists and the Buddhists. Buddhists openly welcome gay people, ordain them, don't consider homosexuality a sin, and have no formal teaching policy on gay and lesbian people. The Unitarian Universalist Association, with more than one thousand congregations nationwide, welcomes gay men and women in all church roles. The Unitarians perform holy unions for gay and lesbian couples, and UU churches across the country offer regular sermons and workshops on gay and lesbian issues, and many individual churches host PFLAG meetings and Metropolitan Community Church congregations (a nationwide church whose membership is primarily gay and lesbian).

> **Why is there so much antagonism between the
> Catholic Church and gay and lesbian people?**

The Catholic Church has been extremely harsh in its condem-
nations of gay and lesbian people and often actively opposes
gay and lesbian rights issues.

In 1990, the National Conference of Catholic Bishops approved a document on human sexuality that labeled homosexual behavior evil but said that gay people themselves were not
sinful. Commenting on the document at the time it was approved, Bishop Edward O'Donnell of St. Louis said, "The ten-
dency or the orientation is a disorder, but the person is not an
evil person."

Beyond this official "love the sinner, hate the sin" policy toward homosexuals, what has most infuriated gay and lesbian
people and gay and lesbian rights supporters has been the in-
sistent opposition of the Catholic Church to gay and lesbian
equal rights, as well as its opposition to AIDS prevention education that involves any mention of condoms.

As if the 1990 document weren't clear enough, in June 1992
the Vatican sent a memo to the leaders of the 57 million Roman
Catholics in the United States reiterating the church's position
that homosexuality is an "objective disorder" and insisting that,
for the sake of the "common good," U.S. bishops oppose legislation barring discrimination against homosexuals in areas that
include adoptions, placement of children in foster care, military
service, and employment of teachers and athletic coaches.

> **Do all Catholics agree with the official church position
> on homosexuality ?**

From what I've written so far, you might get that impression.
And it was that impression that led one reader—whose sister-

in-law is a lesbian—to write a strong letter to me taking issue with the suggestion that all Catholics think one way about gay and lesbian people. She wrote: "Your emphasis may lead to a conclusion that Catholics gain nothing from their religion but homophobia and guilt. I hate to generalize, so I'll simply observe that this isn't true for me. What I get from my religious advisers is almost the opposite. The very word 'Catholic' means accepting everyone. I've learned at church that God doesn't make junk, and this helps me pay no heed to people who would deny human or social rights to gays and lesbians. Attending this year's [1993] march on Washington was an action in profound harmony with my religious beliefs.

"You accurately state that the Church does require gay Catholics to be celibate, much as it requires us not to use birth control (although in practice, both teachings are often honored in the breach). It does not require that we vote in any particular way. . . .

"It would be a shame if anyone concluded they shouldn't come out to a sympathetic friend because the friend is Catholic. Some gay people may need all the friends they can get. I do, too, and some of them are gay."

> **Is the Catholic church the only religious group that has actively opposed the rights of gay and lesbian people?**

Hardly. Many fundamentalist Christian organizations have for years taken a very active role in opposing any efforts to extend equal rights to gay people, effectively demonizing equal rights as "special rights."

One of the most public efforts to express displeasure over the positive treatment of gay people led the Southern Baptist Convention in June 1997 to call for a boycott by its 15.7 million members of the Walt Disney Company, including its theme parks, stores, movie studios, cable television channels, book publishers, trade magazines, newspapers, television and radio stations, and the ABC television network. Southern Baptists were offended by, among other things, Disney's decision to provide health benefits to the partners of gay employees and Disney World "Gay Days," which are organized independently by gay and lesbian groups. Also found to be offensive was ABC television's show *Ellen*, in which the main character came out of the closet as a lesbian, as did Ellen DeGeneres, the actress who played the role.

> ### Has organized religion always opposed homosexuals?

According to historian John Boswell, in his 1980 book *Christianity, Social Tolerance, and Homosexuality*, up until the end of the twelfth century, Christian moral theology treated homosexuality "as, at worst, comparable to heterosexual fornication but more often remained silent on the issue." But then, on the heels of a diatribe from Saint Thomas Aquinas, the church began to view homosexuals as both unnatural and dangerous.

> ### Are there organizations and places of worship specifically for gay people who are religious?

There are organizations all across the country specifically for gay and lesbian people who are Catholic, Jewish, Episcopal, Lutheran—you name it. Also, most major cities have a gay and lesbian synagogue. In addition, the Metropolitan Community Church, whose membership is primarily gay and lesbian, has more than three hundred congregations in the United States and around the world. The largest of the MCC congregations is the twenty-three-hundred-member Cathedral of Hope in Dallas.

> ### Can openly gay people become ministers and rabbis?

More and more openly gay and lesbian people are being ordained as ministers and rabbis, but the entire issue of their ordination has led to heated debates and bitter conflicts across the religious spectrum.

> **How have religious institutions and the clergy been involved in the gay rights effort?**

Some religious institutions and members of the clergy, including the outspokenly progay Episcopal bishop John Shelby Spong, have been very actively involved in supporting the rights of gay and lesbian people.

Perhaps the earliest example of support from religious leaders came in 1965, when a group of liberal ministers, along with local gay rights activists, staged the first major public gay and lesbian fund-raising event in San Francisco for a new organization called the Council on Religion and the Homosexual. The Unitarian Universalists were also gay rights pioneers, in 1970 calling for an end to discrimination against gay and lesbian people in the denomination and in society, declaring that private consensual sexual behavior was a private matter.

> **Can you become heterosexual through prayer?**

Prayer may do a lot of things, but one thing it won't do is make a homosexual into a heterosexual.

It may seem harmless to suggest that prayer is the answer to becoming a heterosexual, but as Mary Griffith, who once held Christian fundamentalist beliefs, discovered, it can be deadly. Griffith believed that if her teenage gay son, Bobby, prayed hard enough, he would become heterosexual.

Bobby prayed, all the while fearing he would be punished by God for his homosexuality. He wrote in his diary, "Why did you do this to me, God? Am I going to hell? That's the gnawing question that's always drilling little holes in the back of my mind. Please don't send me to hell. I'm really not that bad, am I? I want to be good. I want to amount to something. I need your seal of approval. If I had that, I would be happy. Life is so cruel and unfair." A year and a half later, at the age of twenty, Bobby jumped off a highway overpass and landed in the path of an eighteen-wheel truck.

In a letter to other gay young people printed in the *San Francisco Examiner*, Mary Griffith later wrote, "I firmly believe—though I did not, back then—that my son Bobby's suicide is the end result of homophobia and ignorance within most Protestant and Catholic churches, and consequently within society, our public schools, our own family.

"Bobby was not drunk, nor did he use drugs. It's just that we could never accept him for who he was—a gay person.

"We hoped God would heal him of being gay. According to God's word, as we were led to understand it, Bobby had to repent or God would damn him to hell and eternal punishment. Blindly, I accepted the idea that it is God's nature to torment and intimidate us.

"That I ever accepted—believed—such depravity of God toward my son or any human being has caused me much remorse and shame. What a travesty of God's love, for children to grow up believing themselves to be evil, with only a slight inclination toward goodness, and that they will remain undeserving of God's love from birth to death.

"Looking back, I realize how depraved it was to instill false guilt in an innocent child's conscience, causing a distorted image of life, God and self, leaving little if any feeling of personal worth.

"Had I viewed my son's life with a pure heart, I would have recognized him as a tender spirit in God's eyes."

The story of Mary Griffith and Bobby Griffith is chronicled in a compelling book, *Prayers for Bobby: A Mother's Coming to Terms with the Suicide of Her Gay Son*, by Leroy Aarons.

> *What do you say to Christian people who say to gay*
> *people that they love the sinner but hate the sin?*

My simple answer is: Thank you, but I can live without that kind of love.

I think the "love the sinner, hate the sin" philosophy is a convenient way for Christian people who condemn homosexuality to reconcile their feelings about gay men and women. They can feel good about loving the "sinner" and also feel good about not compromising their religious belief's by proclaiming their hatred for the "sin." The problem is, this view assumes that you can separate the alleged sin from the alleged sinner. The fact is, the "sin," my sexual orientation and how I choose to express it, is as much a part of me, the "sinner," as my skin. So if you hate something as fundamental to me as my skin, then you necessarily hate me, too. It's hard to imagine well-meaning people feeling very good about that.

12

?

DISCRIMINATION AND ANTIGAY VIOLENCE

> ### How are gay people discriminated against?

Gay and lesbian people are discriminated against in many different ways. People have, for example, been fired from their jobs, evicted from their homes, and denied custody of their children. Gay and lesbian people are routinely discharged from the military. In many states, gay and lesbian people can be arrested for having sexual relations with another consenting adult in the privacy of their own homes. Gay student groups have been refused official recognition by universities. Gay and lesbian people have been thrown out of fraternities and sororities. Gay boys are not permitted to join the Boy Scouts. Gay and lesbian couples, no matter how many years they have been together, are denied the protections given to nongay married couples. And in a very public case of discrimination in government, President Bill Clinton's nomination of an openly gay man for ambassador to Luxembourg was blocked—and ultimately killed—by three Republican senators who were concerned about the nominee's "gay agenda."

But usually the discrimination experienced by gay people isn't nearly so obvious as being arrested in your bedroom or receiving a pink slip or an eviction notice. More typical is a landlord who won't rent to two "single" men (only to married couples) or a boss who never follows through on a promised job promotion.

> ### How are gay and lesbian people harassed? Does it happen often?

Harassment of gay and lesbian people ranges from name-calling and spray-painting antigay epithets on the homes of gay and lesbian people to slashing tires on cars parked outside gay bars and vandalizing offices of gay and lesbian organizations. Harassment is particularly common among high school and college students, as indicated by two studies conducted in the late 1990s. (For more information on these studies see, "What do heterosexual teenagers think of their gay and lesbian peers?" in chapter 2.)

All too often, antigay incidents go well beyond name-calling to death threats, beatings, and even murder.

> ### Are people really murdered because they're gay?

Indeed they are. In 1996, the latest year for which statistics were available, twenty-one men and women were killed in the United States because of their sexual orientation, according to the Southern Poverty Law Center, an Alabama organization that tracks violence against minorities.

The case that brought the most national attention in recent years was the 1998 murder of Matthew Shepard, a gay University of Wyoming student who was kidnapped, robbed, pistol-whipped, and left tied to a fence for eighteen hours in near-freezing temperatures. His death five days later led to outrage across the country and a call for a national hate-crimes law that would include crimes based on sexual orientation.

> **Is antigay violence a new problem or a big problem?**

Talk to older gay and lesbian people and you quickly discover that antigay violence is nothing new. Barbara Gittings, an early gay rights activist, recalled an incident in the 1950s at a gay bar in New York City: "I was with my friend Pinky. I don't remember why we called him Pinky, but anyway, Pinky got friendly with a couple of uniformed guys who had come into the bar, Marines, I believe. They were sitting and talking with us. When the four of us left the bar, out came the brass knuckles. They proceeded to rip up Pinky's face. They cut open his nose entirely. And they said to me, 'We aren't touching you, Sonny, because you wear glasses.' It was terrifying, and there was not a damn thing I could do until they had finished their dirty work and left. Then I helped Pinky up and got him to a hospital. He had thirteen stitches in his nose. I guess in my innocence I hadn't thought people could be so hateful and violent toward us. Pinky didn't want to report it to the police. He figured they wouldn't do anything about it and they might give him a hard time. He was probably right."

Several early gay rights activists I spoke with talked about how they couldn't call the police after incidents like the one Barbara Gittings described, because, they said, the police were often the ones who did the beating.

Today, the issue of antigay violence is being taken more seriously by public authorities. A number of government reports have concluded that gay and lesbian people are the most frequent victims of hate-motivated violence. Following the passage of the National Hate Crimes Statistics Act in 1990, the federal government began collecting statistics from sixteen thousand police departments on crimes motivated by prejudice, including prejudice based on sexual orientation. According to the Federal Bureau of Investigation, sexual orientation was a factor in 11.6 percent of the 8,759 hate crimes recorded in 1996 (the latest year for which figures were available).

The National Coalition of Anti-Violence Programs, a coalition of twenty-five state and local gay/lesbian/bisexual/transgender tracking programs, reported a 2 percent increase in incidents against lesbian/gay/bisexual/transgender and HIV-positive people between 1996 and 1997. The organization reported a total of 2,445 incidents in 1997 (the latest year for which figures were available). But many of those who monitor these numbers agree that only a small percentage of the victims of antigay attacks report these incidents, because people fear that their sexual orientation will be made public or that their reports won't be taken seriously by the police, or because they fear being abused by the police.

> *Are there organizations that combat antigay violence?*

Yes, several of the organizations that track antigay violence for the National Coalition of Anti-Violence Programs work in their cities and states to combat antigay violence. This includes educating police departments about gay and lesbian people and the problem of antigay violence, working with the police to identify antigay crimes, and working with victims and witnesses to gather information they would otherwise be reluctant to convey directly to the police. Some organizations also send speakers into local high schools to educate students about gay and lesbian people, with the goal of heading off antigay violence.

The National Coalition of Anti-Violence Programs produces an annual report on antigay violence, and the coalition, along with many of the local groups, works at the state and national levels to lobby for hate-crimes laws that include crimes based on sexual orientation.

> ### What are hate-crimes laws, and how can these prevent antigay violence?

Hate-crimes laws generally increase penalties for crimes motivated by prejudice. In other words, someone who assaults a Jewish man because he is Jewish (as evidenced by name-calling, for example) could be charged with a hate crime as well as with assault and battery. Forty-one states and the District of Columbia have hate-crimes laws. Of the forty-two total, twenty have laws that mention race, religion, or ethnicity; eleven, laws that mention sexual orientation; eleven, laws that mention gender; and twelve, laws that mention other categories.

The whole issue of hate-crimes laws is extremely complex and contentious, with some people arguing that such laws are an important tool in prosecuting and deterring hate crimes and others arguing that these laws restrict political speech.

> ### How can someone report antigay violence?

The first thing to do is call the police. You should also call your local gay and lesbian antiviolence organization to report the incident. To find the group nearest to where you live, you can call the New York City Gay and Lesbian Anti-Violence Project, the largest of the antiviolence organizations. The New York City group also publishes an annual report on antigay violence nationwide (see "Resources" for contact information).

> **Why do people discriminate against, harass, and attack gay men and lesbians?**

Some do so because they believe that homosexuality is sinful and immoral or that homosexuals are child molesters, disease carriers, and/or mentally ill. Others believe that homosexuality is contrary to American family values and threatens to destroy the American family. For years, the U.S. military has claimed that gay people were security risks, a threat to morale, and "prejudicial to good order and discipline."

University of California research psychologist Dr. Gregory M. Herek, author of *Hate Crimes: Confronting Violence Against Lesbians and Gay Men*, states that for most people who are biased against gay people, homosexuals "stand as a proxy for all that is evil . . . such people see hating gay men and lesbians as a litmus test for being a moral person."

Other psychologists who have studied antigay bias say it results from a combination of fear and self-righteousness in which gay people are perceived as contemptible threats to the moral universe. Experts also agree that these antigay feelings are often supported by religious institutions that consider homosexuality to be sinful.

There are still other reasons people discriminate against, verbally harass, and physically express their hate for gay men and lesbians. Young people in particular are often motivated by a desire to be a part of the crowd or to gain the approval of their peers or family. Another often-heard explanation for what motivates people who are antigay is fear of their own homosexual feelings. According to Dr. Herek, "Although the explanation probably is used more often than is appropriate, it does apply to some men who will attack gays as a way of denying unacceptable aspects of their own personalities."

When Jean, who describes herself as "not exactly a Marilyn Monroe type," was beaten up several years ago, her attackers made perfectly clear what they didn't like about her: "These four guys were yelling antilesbian remarks: 'Who do you think you are? You wanna look like a man? We'll show you!' That kind of stuff." Jean was walking home from the gym in New York's Greenwich Village. "There was a woman with them, but she didn't say that much. They came up behind me and started kicking a tin can at me. By the time I got to the end of the block, they were kicking it pretty hard, and it was hitting me. So I turned around. I remember saying something like, 'What's the matter here?' And the guy hit me. His first punch broke my nose. The other person hit me in the stomach. I couldn't stand up after that. I fell down. I was already a bloody mess, and then one of them kicked me in the back." Jean suffered a permanent back injury as a result of the attack.

°13

?

SEX

No discussion of sex can begin without addressing the issue of AIDS and doing what's necessary to prevent the spread of HIV, the virus that causes AIDS. For questions on AIDS, see chapter 18, "AIDS." And for the latest information on how to prevent infection with HIV, talk to your doctor, or call a local health organization or local or national AIDS information hot line. The National AIDS Hotline, at 1-800-342-AIDS, is staffed around the clock by information specialists who can answer your questions about AIDS and HIV.

> *What do gay and lesbian people do in bed?*
> *How do gay and lesbian people have sex?*

First, what do we mean by "having sex"? A heterosexual young man who asked me what gay people consider "having sex" told me that for him having sex meant intercourse with a woman. Everything else was "just fooling around." I like using a broader definition. For the purpose of this question, having sex means stimulating each other sexually. And let's not forget the emotional component, because for many people, sex means both physical and emotional intimacy.

There's no mystery about what gay and lesbian people do to stimulate each other sexually, because what gay and lesbian people do is essentially what heterosexuals do. Generally, people do what makes them feel good. That means looking at each other, talking to each other, kissing, holding hands, massaging each other, holding each other, licking each other—in short, stimulating each other in some way that makes them feel aroused. Of course, some things feel better than others, because some parts of the body are naturally more sensitive, like nipples, breasts, buttocks, the clitoris, the penis, the anus, lips, and for some people, that tender spot on the back of the neck. People use all kinds of things to stimulate the parts that feel good, including fingers, hands, tongue, mouth, penis, toes; you name it, people use it.

Having sex may or may not include reaching orgasm. And just as there are all kinds of ways to stimulate each other sexually, there are all kinds of ways to reach orgasm, although reaching orgasm usually requires stimulating the penis (for men), or stimulating the clitoris and/or the G-spot (for women).

> *What about intercourse?*

It's important to note that sexual intercourse—both anal and vaginal—without the use of a condom offers the highest risk of contracting AIDS. So before engaging in sexual intercourse or any other sexual activity with another person, please learn what you need to know about preventing infection with HIV.

(For further information on HIV/AIDS, see chapter 18, "AIDS.")

Two men can, if they choose, have anal intercourse—insertion of the penis of one man into the anus of the other. Some men achieve orgasm in this way.

Two women who desire vaginal penetration can use fingers, toes, a dildo, or whatever feels good to them. Some lesbians who desire the experience of intercourse use a dildo attached to a waist harness that allows one woman to have intercourse with another.

> **How can a lesbian be sexually fulfilled/satisfied (i.e.,
> achieve orgasm) without a penis during intercourse?**

Any woman—gay or nongay—can tell you that you don't need a penis to achieve an orgasm, and that penile-vaginal intercourse does not guarantee an orgasm. What is usually required to achieve orgasm is stimulation of the clitoris, which is located outside and above the vagina, and/or the G-spot, which is located inside the vagina. The clitoris can be stimulated using a number of different things, including fingers, the mouth, or a vibrator. And if a woman desires vaginal stimulation, a penis isn't required, because there are many different ways to penetrate and stimulate the vagina without a penis.

> **Do all gay men regularly engage in anal intercourse?**

No, this is a myth. However, some people—gay and nongay, male and female—find anal stimulation and/or penetration with a penis, fingers, dildo, or whatever, pleasurable. Others don't. And some men—gay and nongay—enjoy inserting their penis into the anus of a partner—male or female. Others don't.

I know this seems like a very short answer to what for many people is a very highly charged issue—moral and otherwise—but I believe that whether or not two people choose to have anal intercourse or one partner stimulates another partner's anus or wants to have his or her anus stimulated is really just a matter of personal preference.

> ### Why do some gay men have anal intercourse while others don't?

Gay men who engage in anal intercourse do so because it gives them pleasure, gives their partner pleasure, or both.

Gay men who don't engage in anal intercourse, either as the one doing the penetrating or the one being penetrated, give a number of different reasons. Some men find it physically uncomfortable to be anally penetrated by a penis, or they don't enjoy assuming what has been traditionally considered a passive role. Other men choose not to engage in anal intercourse because of moral concerns or concerns about cleanliness. Others fear the possibility of contracting AIDS, even with the use of a condom.

> ### Do lesbians use sex toys?
> ### Do gay men use sex toys?

Ask any purveyor of sex toys about who buys and uses the various sexual implements available, and you'll find out that all kinds of people, male and female, gay and nongay, old and young, religious and agnostic, use sex toys.

> ### Do gay men use pornography?
> ### Do lesbians use pornography?

Some do, some don't. But in glancing at the shelves of any store that sells pornographic magazines and sells or rents videotapes, it's easy to see that there's a much larger market for pornography that appeals to gay men than for pornography that appeals to lesbians. And just the same, there is a much larger market for pornography that appeals to heterosexual men than there is for pornography that appeals to heterosexual women.

> **If a lesbian uses a dildo, doesn't that imply that she wants to be with a man?**

No. A lesbian who uses a dildo is simply choosing that type of vaginal or anal stimulation—just as when a heterosexual man uses a dildo for his own anal stimulation it doesn't mean he wants to have intercourse with a man.

> **What are tops and bottoms?**

This distinction, when it's made, is usually made by gay men. When a gay man refers to himself as a "top" or a "bottom," what he's saying is that he prefers to be the one doing the penetrating during anal intercourse—a "top"—or that he prefers to be penetrated—a "bottom." The distinction between tops and bottoms is also made among some lesbians, where a "top" uses a dildo or other implement to penetrate a "bottom."

Some people also use the "top" and "bottom" labels for the person who takes the aggressive versus the passive role when having sex of any kind.

Though some gay men and lesbians strictly define their sexual roles as "tops" or "bottoms," most do not use these labels and are likely to shift from more aggressive to less aggressive roles from minute to minute, hour to hour, day to day, week to week.

> **Is a lesbian's clitoris bigger than that of a heterosexual woman?**

The size of a woman's clitoris is not dependent on her sexual orientation.

> **Do gay men have bigger sexual appetites than
> nongay men?**

The popular myth is that gay men have enormous sexual appetites and have sex all the time. The truth is dull to report. Gay men and heterosexual men are different only in whom they desire, not how much they desire.

> **Are lesbians virgins?**
> **What, for gay men, is considered losing your virginity?**

This question reminds me of a conversation I had with a woman friend in college. Long after she told me about all the fun she'd been having with her new boyfriend, she said she intended to remain a virgin until she married. Boy, was I perplexed! I thought back over our earlier conversations about how her boyfriend had done this to her or how she had done that to him. There was plenty of talk about what I thought sounded like passionate, sweaty, messy, lusty sex. How, I asked her, could she define herself as a virgin after all that sex? "I've never had intercourse," she explained. Oh. After thinking about it, I had to agree that my friend was technically a virgin, but only because she had never had a penis in her vagina. By her own description, her boyfriend's penis had been almost everywhere else.

Using the penile penetration definition of virginity doesn't work quite so well for gay men and lesbians. For example, is a sexually active lesbian who has never had intercourse with a man still a virgin? Is a sexually active gay man who has never been penetrated anally by another man still a virgin? What if he has penetrated another man but never been penetrated himself?

Given the realities and complexities of sexual relations between men and women, men and men, and women and women,

I think it's time for a new definition of virginity. So I vote for the definition that says you are no longer a virgin if you've had sexual relations with another person involving genital stimulation to orgasm.

> **Do gay people in relationships have less sex over time?**

Just like heterosexual couples, most gay and lesbian couples have less sex with each other over time. Among the forty couples I interviewed for my book about happy, long-lasting gay and lesbian relationships, the younger couples—those in their thirties and forties who had been together for nine or more years— were having sex on average one to eight times a month. But the range for all the couples was from no sex at all for a handful of couples to sexual relations of some kind every day for one pair of men who had been together for twenty-five years.

> **Do gay people feel guilty about having sex with each other?**

When I was a young man I felt very guilty about having sex with men. By the time I became sexually active, I knew I preferred men, but I also knew that according to everything I had learned, homosexuality was wrong, so of course I felt guilty about doing something wrong. But my guilt—which obviously didn't stop me, and which faded over time—was nothing compared with the experience of one man who had a relationship with a man who was devoutly Catholic. According to him, "Every time after we had sex, barely a second after my boyfriend had an orgasm, he would be out of bed, on his knees, genuflecting and begging God for forgiveness. I can't believe I managed to put up with that for six months before breaking up with him. He needed help, and I tried, but there was nothing I could do for him."

My experience and that of the devout Catholic is not everyone's experience. As Sonya explained to me, the first time she was with a woman, she didn't feel guilty at all. "Making love to a woman felt like the most perfectly natural thing in the world for me," she said. "I was thirty-two. This is what I wanted. I'd waited all my life for it. Why in heaven's name would I feel guilty? I felt like going out and celebrating!"

> **Can a gay person have sex with someone of the opposite gender?**
> **Is it pleasurable?**

Most gay and lesbian people—although certainly not all—have had sex with someone of the opposite gender. That should come as no surprise, given that that's what we all learned we were supposed to do. And though sex with someone of the opposite gender may not have been our first choice, for many gay and lesbian people there was still pleasure in the experience.

> **Are gay men physically repulsed by women?**
> **Are lesbians physically repulsed by men?**

The fact that you have feelings of sexual attraction for people of the same gender doesn't necessarily mean that you are physically repulsed by the opposite gender. Most gay and lesbian people simply don't have significant feelings of sexual attraction for the opposite gender.

When I first came out to some of my nongay male friends in college, a couple of them assumed I found women physically repulsive. I explained how I felt by telling them a story about my girlfriend in summer camp when I was in my early teens. Eva had brown hair, green eyes, and a beautiful body. She was pretty, fun, and adventuresome. We had a great time together. We even held hands and liked to cuddle. But when the other boys talked about trying to get to first or second base with their girlfriends (this was a long time ago, and none of us even considered the possibility of getting to home plate), I remember thinking that I'd rather play cards. If the other boys hadn't mentioned it, the possibility of getting sexual with Eva never would have occurred to me. But I certainly wasn't repulsed by her.

> *Are gay men promiscuous? Why?*

If you believe what some people say about gay men, you would think that all gay men have had a thousand or more sexual partners by the time they're thirty. Some very sexually active men—gay and nongay—have had a thousand or more sexual partners by the time they're thirty, but most single gay men feel lucky if they can get a date on Saturday night.

Most gay men who have lots of different sexual partners aren't doing it because of a desire to challenge society's general condemnation of promiscuity. They're doing it for a simple reason: They enjoy having a variety of sexual partners.

> *What are gay bathhouses and sex clubs?*
> *Why do gay men go to them?*
> *Do women go to these kinds of places?*

Gay male bathhouses and sex clubs are actually two different things. A gay bathhouse is typically set up like a health club and may have a weight room, a TV room, a sauna, a steam room, a swimming pool, and other amenities. It may also have cubicles with beds that you can rent. When you enter a bathhouse you're assigned a locker, where you put your clothes.

The reason gay men go to bathhouses is generally to have sex, not lift weights. So once your clothes are in your locker, the search for a sexual partner or partners begins. There is no lesbian equivalent of gay male bathhouses.

Sex clubs are designed to appeal to all kinds of people and often don't have a permanent location. In other words, a sex club event may be held at one location this week and another the next week. Some sex clubs are strictly for gay men, some for lesbians (although sex clubs are generally not popular among lesbians), some for both, and some for heterosexual people. In major cities, if you have a sexual desire, you can usually find a sex club where you can satisfy it, no matter what your sexual orientation.

❯ Why do gay men have sex in bathrooms and public parks?

Historically, public parks and rest rooms were just about the only places besides gay bars where men could find other men for sexual encounters. And though frequenting public parks and rest rooms meant risking arrest by undercover police, such places allowed for even greater anonymity than did gay bars. At a time when almost all gay people kept their homosexuality a secret, anonymity was paramount.

Though gay men can now find sexual partners in lots of other places, some continue to seek out and engage in sex in public places. Men who do this give several different reasons for engaging in public sex. Some men find this kind of sexual encounter convenient and quick. As one man explained, "There's no negotiating. You don't have to buy anyone a drink. You don't have to figure out whose home you're going to go to. You don't even have to say a single word." Other men find the sense of danger inherent in public sex to be sexually exciting. Others like watching other men engage in sex. And still others want the anonymity of public sex because they're in a married heterosexual relationship, deeply closeted, or involved in a couple relationship with another man.

> **Do lesbians engage in sex in public rest rooms and public parks?**

In general, lesbians do not engage in public sex. But all kinds of people—gay and nongay, men and women—at one time or another have had sex in public parks, rest rooms, and airplanes, on beaches, and anywhere else you can imagine.

14

?

THE MASS MEDIA: MOVIES, TELEVISION, PRINT

> Has Hollywood portrayed gay people accurately?
> Why do gay people protest movies that portray gay men and lesbians in a negative way?

Gay and lesbian people—individually, through organized protests, and through the Gay and Lesbian Alliance Against Defamation (GLAAD)—have complained plenty about how they've been portrayed by Hollywood, and with good reason. Until recent years, almost without exception, gay and lesbian people have been portrayed in mainstream Hollywood movies as murderers, twisted villains, victims, or wimps. For a long time it was difficult to get through a movie without someone making an antigay joke or using offensive words like *fag* and *dyke*. And though these days gay people don't feel compelled to kill themselves onscreen as often as they once did, they still blow out their brains every now and then. All this is thoroughly documented by the late film historian Vito Russo in his book *The Celluloid Closet: Homosexuality in the Movies*.

When I've been asked this question in the past and offered the above answer, people usually note that Hollywood has portrayed every ethnic, racial, religious, or other kind of group in a negative way at one time or another. True, but Hollywood movies have also portrayed these people in positive ways as well, so at least there's some balance. When it comes to gay and lesbian people, for most of Hollywood's history there has rarely been any attempt to portray them in a realistic and balanced manner.

Fortunately, things in Hollywood have been changing in recent years. Positive gay and lesbian characters are hardly commonplace in mainstream Hollywood films, but they have been featured in a growing number of movies, including Paul Rudnick's hilarious *In & Out*, *My Best Friend's Wedding*, *The Object of My Affection*, and *As Good As It Gets*.

> **But aren't there a lot of movies that portray gay and lesbian people positively?**

Yes, but almost all of these movies have been produced independently. The list of wonderful independent movies that feature gay and lesbian characters and story lines grows every day. Some of my favorites include *Gods and Monsters*, *The Opposite of Sex*, *The Wedding Banquet*, *I Think I Do*, and *The Adventures of Priscilla, Queen of the Desert*. I checked in with one of my close lesbian friends for her favorites, and these include *Go Fish*, *The Incredibly True Adventures of Two Girls in Love*, *When Night is Falling*, *French Twist*, and *All Over Me*.

Has television portrayed gay people accurately?

Not long ago, I caught an episode of *Lost in Space,* a 1960s television show I watched religiously when I was a kid. I was stunned to realize as an adult that one of the show's main characters, Dr. Smith, was clearly played as a stereotypical gay man. He was effeminate, timid, and physically weak. But that wasn't all. He was also duplicitous, scheming, selfish, and downright evil. Week after week he put the lives of the other characters at risk as he sought to enrich himself, fill his stomach, or find his way back to Earth. Not exactly a fine role model.

For most of its history, television simply ignored gay and lesbian people, except for the occasional Dr. Smith–style homosexual. In later years, homosexuality was treated as a "special issue," or the story line was about a gay man with AIDS.

Gay characters first began appearing on single episodes of network television shows in the early 1970s—including an episode of the *Mary Tyler Moore Show.* And the first regularly appearing gay character—played by Billy Crystal—hit the airwaves in the late 1970s on ABC's *Soap.* But in general, it wasn't until the 1990s that gay men and women were simply absorbed into a script without much of a fuss. By the end of the decade, more than twenty supporting gay and lesbian characters were scattered throughout the prime-time television schedule, on shows ranging from *Mad About You* and *Friends* to *Melrose Place* and *Dawson's Creek.*

The biggest fuss in the late 1990s was made in 1997 over the coming out of Ellen Morgan, television's first prime-time lesbian lead character, played by comedian Ellen DeGeneres, who herself came out at the same time. The special hourlong coming-out episode of *Ellen* drew an audience of more than 40 million viewers, including many gay and lesbian people who attended special fund-raising viewing parties. I attended one of those parties, and thought the episode was wonderfully written and hilarious. A year later, ABC television canceled *Ellen*, citing declining ratings.

The end of *Ellen* did not, however, mean the end of a gay lead character on television. The 1998 television season saw the launch of *Will & Grace*, a show about a gay man and his female heterosexual best friend.

> **Why do advertisers sometimes object to gay characters or themes on TV?**

Advertisers traditionally avoid being associated with any controversial topic, particularly homosexuality. They fear turning off potential customers and don't want to invite the wrath of antigay activists through product boycotts, for example. Because of this fear, advertisers sometimes pull their sponsorship from shows they object to.

> **Why do gay people have their own magazines and newspapers?**
> **When did the first magazines published by gay people appear?**
> **What did newspapers and magazines say about gay people in the 1950s and 1960s and earlier?**

Gay and lesbian publications offer two things that mass-market, mainstream publications can't. First, they provide gay and lesbian readers with the kind of in-depth news and information they want about issues that concern them and that they aren't likely to find anywhere else. Second, they serve advertisers trying to reach a gay and lesbian market.

When the first gay and lesbian magazines were published in the 1950s, they were just about the only places where gay and lesbian people could read anything about themselves that didn't include such headlines as "Nest of Perverts Raided," "How L.A. Handles Its 150,000 Perverts," "Great Civilizations Plagued by Deviates," and "Pervert Colony Uncovered in Simpson

Slaying Probe." Although these newspaper headlines actually appeared in mainstream newspapers in the mid-1950s, most often, gay and lesbian people were simply ignored.

Stories on gay and lesbian people appeared with increasing frequency in the mainstream press through the 1960s and 1970s, but most of the coverage continued to be biased against gay people. One of my favorite examples comes from an unsigned essay in the January 21, 1966, issue of *Time* magazine. The essay, entitled "The Homosexual in America," stated: "For many a woman with a busy or absent husband, the presentable homosexual is in demand as an escort—witty, pretty, catty, and no problem to keep at arm's length. . . . The once widespread view that homosexuality is caused by heredity, or some derangement of hormones, has been generally discarded. The consensus is that it is caused psychically, through a disabling fear of the opposite sex."

The essay noted that both male and female homosexuality were "essentially a case of arrested development, a failure of learning, a refusal to accept the full responsibilities of life. This is no more apparent than in the pathetic pseudo marriages in which many homosexuals act out conventional roles—wearing wedding rings, calling themselves 'he' and 'she.'" The essayist saved the best for last: "[Homosexuality] is a pathetic little second-rate substitute for reality, a pitiable flight from life. As such it deserves fairness, compassion, understanding and when possible, treatment. But it deserves no encouragement, no glamorization, no rationalization, no fake status as minority martyrdom, no sophistry about simple differences in taste—and above all, no pretense that it is anything but a pernicious sickness."

Today, many mainstream publications are doing a fine job of accurately reporting major gay and lesbian stories, but no matter how good they get, mass-market newspapers and magazines can't offer gay and lesbian readers and advertisers what local and national special-market publications can.

> ### *Are there openly gay journalists?*

Plenty, and this has in no small part led to a quiet revolution in reporting on gay and lesbian people and issues. As more and more journalists, editors, and producers have come out of the closet about their sexual orientation, they have helped their news organizations—from newspapers and magazines to broadcast television and cable—more accurately report on gay and lesbian people and issues. (See, "Resources" for contact information on the National Lesbian & Gay Journalists Association.)

> ### *Are there a lot of books published just for gay and lesbian people?*

The publication of books written for gay and lesbian people has become big business as the publishing industry has discovered what independent gay and lesbian publishers have known for some time: Gay and lesbian people read just like everyone else and, in fact, buy more books than the average reader. Just to give you an idea of the phenomenal growth of gay publishing, in 1979 only about 150 books were published on topics specifically geared for the gay and lesbian market. Twenty years later, the annual number of new titles for that market was closing in on 2,000.

The first bookstore specifically for gay and lesbian people, the Oscar Wilde Memorial Bookshop, opened in 1967 in New York City's Greenwich Village. Today there are dozens of such stores across the country that stock thousands of books written specifically for gay men and women. Also, many independent and chain bookstores maintain special gay and lesbian sections.

15

?

SPORTS

> *Why don't gay men like sports?*

Okay, I admit it. I don't like competitive sports and couldn't care less which baseball or football team is in first place. So I should have known I was gay after the tenth time I struck out playing baseball in summer camp, right? But what about the gay male friend of mine who flies from city to city to follow his favorite football team and is an avid triathlete? And how do you explain the thousands of gay men who participate in the Gay Games (see "What are the Gay Games?" later in this chapter), not to mention the many closeted gay male professional athletes?

The fact is, lots of men are good at and/or like sports, and that includes lots of gay men. And plenty of men are bad at and/or don't like sports, and that includes plenty of heterosexual men. Are gay men more likely to be bad at and/or dislike sports than heterosexual men? Possibly, but until someone figures out a way to survey the largely invisible and hidden gay population, we won't know the answer for sure.

> **Are all women athletes and physical education teachers lesbians?**

One of the classic stereotypes about lesbians is that all of them are good athletes. Indeed, there are women athletes and physical education teachers who are lesbians, but there are also plenty of lesbians like my friend Linda, who can't throw a ball or swing a golf club to save her life. And, of course, there are plenty of women athletes and physical education teachers who are heterosexual.

According to Dr. Dee Mosbacher, a psychiatrist who produced a video on homophobia and women in sports, the question isn't how many lesbian women are in sports, but why some people are playing into the public's fear of homosexuality and accusing women in sports of being lesbians. "The charge of lesbianism," explained Dr. Mosbacher, "is used for several reasons. For example, when recruiting women athletes for college, some coaches have tried to attract certain women by suggesting that the coach at a competing school is a lesbian. And the charge of lesbianism has also been used to discourage or avoid hiring female coaches. As women's sports have become significantly more lucrative in recent years, and more men have been competing for coaching jobs, we've seen an increase in this kind of accusation against women coaches."

> **What are the Gay Games?**

The first International Gay Athletic Games were held from August 29 through September 5, 1982, in San Francisco. More than thirteen hundred athletes from fifteen countries participated. The 1994 Gay Games in New York City attracted more than fifteen thousand athletes from forty countries. In 1998, the Gay Games took place in Europe for the first time, in Amsterdam. Nearly 15,000 athletes from seventy-eight countries participated.

The Gay Games were originally named the Gay Olympics, but the U.S. Olympic Committee, which by act of Congress owns the word *Olympic*, brought a lawsuit prior to the first Gay Games and succeeded in preventing the event's organizers from using the word. And this was despite the fact there had been many other legally unquestioned "Olympics" for all kinds of things, including Olympics for dogs, frogs, and hamburger chefs.

The purpose of the Gay Games, according to a Gay Games spokesperson, is to "hold a true Olympic event, open to all participants, whose goal is to do their personal best. The event is sponsored by the lesbian and gay community to celebrate lesbians and gay men and promote our self-esteem, pride, and dignity."

The Gay Games were founded by Dr. Tom Waddell, a 1968 U.S. Olympic decathlete. (Waddell also helped organize the famous protest by black U.S. athletes at the 1968 Summer Olympics in Mexico City.) He died from AIDS in 1987.

> *Are there any openly gay star athletes?*

Very few professional athletes—star or otherwise—have come out of the closet during or after their careers. The list of professional athletes who have come out is short and includes tennis superstar Martina Navratilova, four-time Olympic gold medalist Greg Louganis, the 1996 U.S. figure-skating champion Rudy Galindo, former San Francisco 49er running back Dave Kopay, golfer Muffin Spencer-Devlin, former Oakland A's outfielder

Glenn Burke, former Mr. America and Mr. Universe Bob Paris, Wimbledon tennis champion Conchita Martinez, up-and-coming French tennis star Amelie Mauresmo, who came out in 1999 after her first Grand Slam Final, swimmer Bruce Hayes, who won a gold medal at the 1984 Summer Olympics in the 800-meter freestyle relay and seven gold medals at the 1990 Gay Games, and Australian soccer player Ian Roberts, who came out in 1994 while he was still an active competitor.

> ### *Why aren't there more openly gay athletes?*

Professional athletes fear risking their careers, as well as lucrative product endorsements, should their homosexuality become public knowledge. And their fears are not unfounded. Former 49er Dave Kopay couldn't get any job in football after he came out publicly in 1975. Kopay had hoped to coach on the college level, but he couldn't find anyone willing to hire him at any level, so he went to work at his uncle's floor-covering store in Hollywood.

Even for a seemingly untouchable high-profile star like tennis great Martina Navratilova, there is a price to pay for being honest. Besides being accused by former tennis champion Margaret Court of ruining the sport and setting a bad example for younger players, Navratilova has said in interviews that being open about her sexual orientation has led to her receiving fewer offers for product endorsements.

16

?

EDUCATION

> *What do students learn about homosexuality in
> elementary school and high school?*

Students learn plenty about homosexuality in school, almost
all of it informally, and nearly all of it bad. The first lesson
occurs when one child calls another a fag in the elementary
school cafeteria, and the lessons continue right on through
high school, when a group of students decides to torment a
theater teacher they think is gay.

Formal education about homosexuality is more remarkable
for what isn't said than for what is said, because with few exceptions, almost nothing is said. School curricula are virtually
devoid of gay subjects. The half-century history of the gay civil
rights movement doesn't come up in social studies lessons that

include discussions about women's rights and black civil rights. Historical and contemporary figures—authors, artists, politicians, and so on—who are gay are rarely if ever identified as such. High school history textbooks mention not a word about gay and lesbian anything. If a school district has an official policy about teaching gay and lesbian issues, that policy is more often than not to forbid the mention of gay and lesbian people and issues in any positive context.

There are, however, exceptions. Several of the nation's largest school districts have policies that protect gay, lesbian, bisexual, and transgender students and staff from discrimination and harassment, provide workshops for teachers on gay, lesbian, bisexual, and transgender youth issues, and have incorporated the lives and accomplishments of gay and lesbian people into the curriculum.

The various national education organizations, including the two largest teachers' unions, have also been supportive of educating students about gay and lesbian people, helping teachers learn how to talk about homosexuality, and making counseling available to gay and lesbian teens. In general, these efforts have been very slow to trickle down to the local level, where the majority of individual school boards are politically conservative.

Still, for the most part, and for the vast majority of schools in the country, what little teaching is done about gay and lesbian people is done by individual teachers in individual high school classes, usually in the context of English, health, or social studies lessons.

> ### Are there any organizations working to change this?

Yes. Since its start in the early 1990s, the Gay, Lesbian & Straight Education Network (GLSEN) has become a driving force in changing how schools deal with the gay and lesbian issue, in terms of both what students are taught about homosexuality and how gay, lesbian, bisexual, and transgender students are treated. The official "mission" of the organization is "to assure that each member of every school community is valued and respected, regardless of sexual orientation. We believe that such an atmosphere engenders a positive sense of self, which is the basis of educational achievement and personal growth. We welcome as members any and all individuals, regardless of sexual orientation or occupation, who are committed to seeing this philosophy realized in K–12." Beginning in the early 1990s with a single chapter, GLSEN has grown to the point where there are now ninety chapters across the country, with a total membership of more than ten thousand.

GLSEN works as an advocate with mainstream education organizations, including the National Education Association and the American Federation of Teachers (the two largest national teachers' unions) and the National School Board Association, on issues ranging from the implementation of nondiscrimination policies that specifically mention sexual orientation to the provision of training and workshops for school staff on the issues faced by gay youth.

Perhaps the most exciting thing GLSEN does—in my eyes, anyway—is work directly with high school students across the country through its Student Pride Program, which aids in the "creation and maintenance of gay/straight alliances [GSAs] and similar student groups." The first high school gay/straight alliance was started in 1991 by Kevin Jennings, a history teacher at the Concord Academy, a private high school in Concord, Massachusetts. Jennings started the group with the goal of providing a supportive and safe forum for open discussion between gay and nongay students about the issues gay students were facing in school, with their families, and with their communities. The group was open to all students, and no student had to identify his or her own orientation. (Jennings had started GLSEN in 1990.)

As of early 1999, more than five hundred GSAs, from New York to Utah to Alaska, were registered with GLSEN's Student Pride Program, which, among other things, publishes a newsletter for the GSAs and provides e-mail list-serves and on-line support. (See "Resources" for contact information.)

> **Doesn't Massachusetts have a special statewide law specifically for gay and lesbian students?**

Massachusetts is one of three states—the other two are Connecticut and Wisconsin—to pass a statewide law protecting students from discrimination and harassment based on sexual orientation. Of the three, Massachusetts has been the most active in providing the services necessary to implement its policy on the local level. The state's Department of Safe Schools for Gay Youth coordinates regional training across the state to help staff understand the issues facing gay, lesbian, bisexual, and transgender youth, from name-calling and harassment to physical assault.

> **Do colleges teach courses about homosexuality?**

According to the National Gay and Lesbian Task Force, which keeps track of these things, more than ninety colleges and universities offer at least one course on some aspect of homosexuality. Here's just a sample of course titles from around the country: Sexual Orientation and the Law, Gay and Lesbian Issues in the Workplace, Selected Issues in Human Sexuality, Studies in Gay and Bisexual Literature, and Gay Literature and Film.

At least two dozen colleges and universities have established lesbian and gay studies programs, although depending on the school, these programs have a variety of names, including Lesbian, Gay, Bisexual, Transgender Studies; Lesbian and Gay Studies; Gender/Sexuality Studies; and Queer Studies. Schools that have such programs include Allegheny College; Brown University; City University of New York; Cornell University; San Francisco City College; San Francisco State University; Stanford; University of California, Berkeley; University of Iowa, Iowa City; and the University of Wisconsin, Milwaukee.

Besides formal courses, college students may first hear about homosexuality during orientation—when all kinds of things are discussed, from where to find a good pizza to how to prevent HIV infections. Gay and lesbian issues also come up in a variety of courses from English literature to history.

> ### What objections do people have to teaching students about homosexuality?

I've heard and read just about every objection made to teaching students anything about gay and lesbian people, whether it's teaching about gay and lesbian parents or providing straightforward information about AIDS. Usually these objections have been expressed by an enraged parent at the top of his or her lungs: "You're trying to recruit our children!"; "You want to promote the gay lifestyle!"; "How can you teach little children about sick and perverted behavior?"; "God created Adam and Eve, not Adam and Steve!" And on and on and on.

But as I explain in chapter 1, "The Basics," and in chapter 11, "Religion," gay and lesbian people do not recruit, do not promote the "gay lifestyle," and are not by nature sick and perverted; and many people, including a number of religious leaders, believe that God created gay people just as he created nongay people, and loves them just the same.

Every objection confirms for me the importance of teaching children the truth about gay and lesbian people, because it's clear from what I've heard that many parents are going to bestow on a new generation the old stereotypes, archaic myths, and ancient fears.

> ### Are there high schools especially for gay and lesbian teens?

There are three high schools for gay, lesbian, bisexual, and transgender students: the Harvey Milk School in New York City, the Walt Whitman School in Dallas, and the Eagle Center in Los Angeles. These are special, alternative high schools for small groups of students who, for any number of reasons, are having difficulty attending mainstream high schools.

The Harvey Milk School, for example, which opened in 1985 and is the oldest of the three schools, is run by the Hetrick-Martin Institute, a nonprofit organization that provides counseling and other services to gay, lesbian, bisexual, and transgender youth. It's fully accredited by the New York City Board of Education and is located in several rooms of the institute's headquarters in lower Manhattan.

The few dozen students who attend Harvey Milk are kids who had trouble surviving at regular high schools. They were teased about the way they acted or the way they dressed; in some cases they were beaten and abused. The purpose of the Harvey Milk High School is to reintegrate these students into traditional schools or, failing that, to provide them with a safe place where they can come to terms with their lives and get their high school diplomas.

> ### Are there openly gay and lesbian schoolteachers?

At the college level there are many, at least compared with the late 1970s, when I was in college and there were virtually none. But in K–12 there are comparatively few, for the simple reason that teachers work with children, and given the still significant prejudice—especially when it comes to gay people working with children—they fear for their jobs.

> **Do gay and lesbian teachers influence their students to become homosexual?**
> **Are gay and lesbian teachers bad role models?**

Gay and lesbian teachers can't influence their students to become homosexual any more than heterosexual teachers can influence their students to become heterosexual. That's because you can't make someone gay, lesbian, bisexual, or heterosexual. Openly gay and lesbian teachers can, however, be positive role models to all kids—gay and nongay—just as heterosexual teachers can be positive role models to all kids.

Jim teaches in New York City and makes no effort to hide the fact that he's gay, nor does he make an effort to hide his frustration with parents who object to his presence in the classroom: "First of all, I don't talk about being gay all the time. What do these parents think I do, walk into class and first thing announce I'm gay and have a lover? It makes me crazy! But if it comes up, I'm not gonna lie about it. And when it's in the news, the kids wanna talk about it. They have questions. Should I tell them to go read a book because I'm not allowed to talk about it, because if I talk about it they'll wanna be gay like me? These parents need to get an education. Look, telling the truth about homosexuals doesn't hurt anyone. I'm educating the straight kids by letting them see a teacher who happens to be gay and does a good job. And the gay and lesbian kids get to see that you can be honest about who you are and have a life and a good career."

Do Jim and other openly gay and lesbian teachers, just by their example, encourage more gay and lesbian young people to come out of the closet? There's every reason to believe that this is the case. But what's the alternative? Should we encourage kids to stay in the closet, hide who they are, and pretend to be heterosexual?

> *Are there libraries and archives about gay subjects?*

A number of libraries around the country, including the San Francisco Public Library and the New York Public Library, as well as several university libraries, have—and are in the process of building—substantial gay and lesbian collections.

> *Are women's colleges all lesbian?*

I put this question to a lesbian friend who recently attended a prestigious all-women's college. Her answer: "Unfortunately, no. I don't even think it's disproportionate." However, some colleges and universities give the impression of having more gay and lesbian students because they offer the kind of supportive community in which gay and lesbian students can feel greater freedom to come out of the closet.

17

?

POLITICS, ACTIVISM, AND GAY AND LESBIAN RIGHTS

> *Is homosexuality against the law?*

It is not against the law to be a gay or lesbian person; there are no laws against feelings of attraction. However, twenty U.S. states have "sodomy laws" that make it illegal for gay and lesbian adults to "perform or submit to any sexual act involving the sex organs of one person and the mouth or anus of another." In five of these states, sodomy laws apply only to people of the same gender. But in the remaining fifteen states that have sodomy laws, sexual acts involving the sex organs of one person and the mouth or anus of the other are against the law for both homosexual and heterosexual people. These laws are rarely enforced, but when they are, it is almost exclusively in cases involving sex between two men. If these laws were uniformly and aggressively enforced, almost the entire sexually active adult populations of several states would be in jail.

Until 1961, all states had laws prohibiting sodomy. Since that time, more than half the states have removed these laws through either legislative action or court decisions. But though plenty of progress has already been made by both gay and nongay people to repeal these archaic laws, the Supreme Court in 1987 upheld the right of states to outlaw sexual acts between two people of the same gender.

> **If sodomy laws are rarely enforced, why are gay and lesbian activists working to overturn them?**

Although sodomy laws are indeed rarely enforced, gay and lesbian rights advocates argue that these laws encourage discrimination and hate crimes against gay and lesbian people and can be used to restrict career and employment opportunities. For example, before the Texas appeals court ruled in 1992 that the Texas sodomy law was unconstitutional, the Dallas Police Department used it to deny employment to a lesbian applicant. And the fact remains that gay people have been arrested, however rarely, for having physical relations in the privacy of their own homes.

> **Why do gay and lesbian people feel they need laws to protect them from discrimination?**

The newspaper headlines from the past decade say plenty: "Justices Leave Intact Anti-Gay Measure," "House Approves Measure Barring Gay Adoptions in Washington," "Perot Ends Benefits for Partners of Newly Hired Gay Workers," "Maine Voters Repeal a Law on Gay Rights," "Sex with Boyfriend Costs Gay Man Custody," "Discriminating Against Gay Workers Doesn't Violate a U.S. Law," "Writer Ousted After Saying He's Homosexual,"

"Recognition Is Refused for Gay Alumni," "Fraternity Rebuff to Homosexual Stirring a Whirlwind in Vermont," "Texas Judge Eases Sentence for Killer of 2 Homosexuals," "Judge Rules Scouts Can Block Gay Man as a Troop Leader," "Homosexual, a U.S. Resident 19 Years, Faces Deportation," "Curbs Imposed on Homosexuals as Foster Parents," "Court Rejects Visiting Rights for Former Lesbian Partner."

These headlines offer a few examples of some of the reasons gay and lesbian activists are working for equal rights on the federal, state, and local level. Although life for gay and lesbian people has improved significantly since the gay rights effort began in the 1950s, it is still perfectly legal in most parts of the country to fire gay men and women from their jobs, evict them from their homes, deny them service at restaurants and hotels, and, in many states, arrest them in their own bedrooms for making love with their spouses.

The good news is, gay and lesbian people are currently protected by laws that forbid discrimination in employment, housing, and public accommodation in ten states and scores of municipalities. (The first city to protect the rights of gay people in employment, housing, and public accommodation was Ann Arbor, Michigan, in July 1972.) Major corporations, such as Levi Strauss, AT&T, IBM, and Disney, have also adopted policies forbidding discrimination against gay and lesbian people in hiring and promotions. And federal employees are also protected against discrimination based on sexual orientation.

> ### What are the arguments against giving gay and lesbian people equal rights?

People who oppose the passage of gay and lesbian equal rights laws at the local, state, and federal level give all kinds of reasons. Some argue that gay men and women are not a class of people—like people classified by race or gender—but simply individuals who engage in sick and sinful behavior, and that such behavior shouldn't be protected by law.

I remember sitting through hearings at New York City Hall for local gay rights legislation in the early 1980s, listening to a city councilman claim that if gay people were given equal rights, the city would be encouraging bestiality and child molestation. Seated in the row behind me was a group of devoutly religious men who shouted "Burn them" every time a gay or lesbian person or supporter came up to the podium to testify. I thought these men, many of whom carried copies of the Bible and had relatives who had died in Hitler's gas chambers, made a very compelling case in favor of passing equal rights protection for gay and lesbian people.

Other people argue that gay men and women, like all people, are already guaranteed equal protection under the law by the Constitution and therefore don't need any "special rights." I wholeheartedly agree that gay and lesbian people don't need any special rights—and no one has asked for them—but we certainly need equal rights.

The fact remains that in most places in the nation, gay and lesbian people do not have equal protection under the law. For example, let's say the company I work for decides to fire me because I'm gay. They've been happy with my work and just gave me a raise. But they found out from one of my colleagues that I'm gay and the company doesn't want gay employees. At the same time they fire me, they decide to fire one of my colleagues because they've decided that they don't want Jewish people working for the company any longer. In most places in the United States I would have no recourse, because in most places it is perfectly legal to fire someone simply because they're gay or lesbian. I could not sue my employer to regain my job. My colleague, on the other hand, could sue, because federal civil rights laws forbid discrimination based on religion, among other things.

All that gay and lesbian people are asking for are the same legal protections most Americans take for granted, including protection from discrimination in employment, housing, and public accommodation. These are not "special rights," and the people who promote this antigay "special rights" argument know that gay and lesbian people are working for "equal rights." But the "special rights" argument has nevertheless proven effective in defeating and repealing gay rights legislation, because no one wants any group of people to have "special rights."

One of my favorite arguments from people who say that gay and lesbian people are asking for "special rights" is that gay men in particular are already so successful—apparently we all drive expensive cars and live in sprawling, well-appointed homes—that we couldn't possibly need any extra protection.

> ### Do gay people discriminate?

Gay and lesbian people discriminate in all the ways that heterosexual people do, based on race, gender, physical appearance, age—you name it.

I like the observation made by Martin Block, an early gay activist, about bias among the gay men in his organization, the Mattachine Society, in the early 1950s: "Anytime there was a proposal to do something public, people argued, 'Well, I don't want those drag queens coming' or 'I don't want that one coming' or 'Isn't she outrageous with her constant swish?' I'm not saying that drag queens were not welcome. I'm saying that they were not welcome by everybody. In every gay movement there has always been a schism. Some people don't want anyone who sticks his little pinkie out, and some people don't want anyone who doesn't stick his little pinkie out. None of us is without bias. And I am delighted to say that I am full of bias myself, but my bias is mostly against stupidity."

> ### When did the gay civil rights movement start?

The struggle for gay and lesbian equal rights began in California in the 1950s with the formation of a number of organizations, including the Mattachine Society, founded in Los Angeles in 1950, and the Daughters of Bilitis, an organization for lesbians founded in San Francisco in 1955. These fledgling groups had very modest goals that were a reflection of their tiny memberships, their modest resources, the intensely anti-gay climate of the times, and the overwhelming fear almost all gay and lesbian people had of being found out.

Other than providing discussion groups where gay and lesbian people could meet one another and talk about the problems they faced, these organizations fought for the right of gay and lesbian people to assemble in bars without being harassed or arrested by the police, and they published the first widely circulated magazines for gay and lesbian people.

> ### Wasn't the Stonewall riot in New York City in 1969 the beginning of the gay rights movement?

When I first began work on Making History, my book about the history of the gay and lesbian rights struggle, I thought, like most other gay people, that the gay rights movement began in June 1969 with a riot that followed a routine police raid at the Stonewall Inn, a gay bar in New York City's Greenwich Village.

Soon after I started my research, however, I discovered that by the time of the Stonewall riot, there was already a national, active movement of more than forty gay and lesbian organizations. Though the Stonewall riot was not the beginning, it was, without question, a major turning point in the struggle. It dramatically energized the gay and lesbian rights movement and inspired the formation of scores of new gay and lesbian rights groups across the country.

> ### Why do gay people speak about "gay pride"?

Being proud of one's sexual orientation may seem strange to nongay people, for whom sexual orientation is a relative non-issue. But as Ann Northrop, an activist who has spoken widely on gay and lesbian rights issues, explained to me, "Homosexuals are taught from preconsciousness to be ashamed of themselves and to hate themselves and to think that they are disgusting, aberrant, immoral human beings. So the achievement of any kind of self-esteem in a lesbian or gay person is an incredible victory against almost insurmountable odds in the society we live in. Those of us who have achieved any small measure of self-esteem celebrate and take pride in the extent to which we've been able to achieve it. When you've been given the exact opposite all your life, there is a great need to achieve a sense of pride."

Northrop pointed out that heterosexual people, too, express pride in their heterosexuality, whether or not they realize it, by having weddings, wearing wedding rings, or placing marriage announcements in newspapers. "What is a wedding except a prideful celebration of heterosexuality?" she added.

> ### Why do gay people have marches every year in June?

The annual gay and lesbian marches and celebrations, which are held in cities across the United States and in other countries around the world most often during the month of June, commemorate the June 28, 1969, Stonewall riot. Beyond this shared anniversary, each local committee sets its own theme, which may range from gay and lesbian freedom to gay and lesbian pride. In addition, each of the thousands of individual groups has its own reasons for participating. And the hundreds of thousands of people who take part in the parades and celebrations have their own reasons as well. Some people participate as a show of political strength, to celebrate gay and lesbian pride, to demand equal rights, or all of the above. Others participate to express support for their gay and lesbian children or parents, or to celebrate freedom from the confines of the closet. Others still are there just to have a good time. One young woman, who has been marching in New York City's gay and lesbian parade for the past three years, gave this reason for marching: "It's the one day a year I can walk down the street in broad daylight with my arm around my lover's shoulder and get cheered for it instead of having people spit at us."

Today's gay and lesbian marches and celebrations are a direct descendent of an annual protest march first held on July 4, 1965, in front of Independence Hall in Philadelphia. The annual picket was staged by a couple of dozen very courageous lesbians and gay men who carried signs demanding equal rights for homosexuals.

Martha Shelley, a major gay rights leader in the late 1960s and early 1970s, participated in the Independence Hall protest two years in a row. "I thought it was something that might possibly have an effect," she recalled. "I remember walking around in my little white blouse and skirt and tourists standing there eating their ice-cream cones and watching us like the zoo had opened."

Though most Americans have now seen gay and lesbian people on television, in newspaper and magazine photographs, and in person, when the Independence Hall protests were started, most people had never seen anyone who they knew was a living, breathing homosexual.

The Independence Hall annual picket continued through 1969, the year of the Stonewall riot. The following year, the July 4 Independence Hall picket was discontinued. Instead, a few thousand protesters marched in New York City on June 28 to commemorate the Stonewall riot, celebrate gay pride, and demand equal rights. Over a thousand protesters also marched that same day in Los Angeles.

> **Does the gay rights movement have its own Rosa Parks?**

Though there is only one Rosa Parks, the late Dr. Evelyn Hooker, a pioneering research psychologist, has been called by some people "the Rosa Parks of the gay rights movement."

Dr. Hooker, who was heterosexual, conducted a courageous study in the 1950s in which she compared the psychological profiles of thirty homosexual men and thirty heterosexual men. Dr. Hooker concluded that, contrary to the widely held belief that homosexuality was a mental illness, there were no significant differences between the two groups. Her findings ultimately led to the removal of homosexuality from the American Psychiatric Association's list of mental illnesses in 1973. This change in classification was one of the most important steps in the struggle for gay and lesbian equal rights.

> **What kinds of political organizations do gay and lesbian people have?**

There are all kinds of organizations dedicated to working for gay and lesbian equal rights, from high school and college student groups and political action committees to legal organizations and political clubs. Among the most prominent national groups are: Gay and Lesbian Alliance Against Defamation (GLAAD), Human Rights Campaign (HRC), Lambda Legal Defense and Education Fund, National Gay and Lesbian Task Force (NGLTF), and Parents, Families, and Friends of Lesbians and Gays (PFLAG). (See "Resources" for additional organizations and contact information.)

> **Why do some gay and lesbian people wear a pink triangle?**

A pink inverted triangle symbol (point down) was first used by the Nazis during World War II to identify homosexuals in concentration camps. (Jews had to wear a yellow star of

David.) During the 1970s, as more became known about the persecution and murder of thousands of homosexuals by the Nazis, gay and lesbian people began wearing the pink inverted triangle symbol to publicly identify themselves as homosexuals, as a symbol of pride, and as a way of commemorating those who died in the concentration camps.

> **Why do some gay and lesbian people fly a rainbow flag and display the rainbow symbol on their cars?**

It seems like rainbows are everywhere. Not just flags flown from front porches and decals on car bumpers and windows, but rainbow necklaces, rings, T-shirt insignia, towels, coffee mugs—you name it. It all started with the six-stripe rainbow flag, designed and made in 1978 by San Franciscan Gilbert Baker. His simple, subtle, and colorful symbol of gay and lesbian pride has been adopted around the world. In my own New York City neighborhood, the rainbow flag and rainbow decals are displayed in store windows to let gay and lesbian customers know that their patronage is more than welcome.

> **Are all gay and lesbian people liberals?**

Because the vast majority of visible and politically active gay and lesbian people are relatively liberal, there is the mistaken impression that all gay and lesbian people are Democrats and support liberal causes. But, in fact, there are plenty of gay and lesbian people who identify themselves as Republicans and more than a few gay men and women who are very conservative, including the late Marvin Liebman, a founder of the modern conservative movement.

> **Is it true that the FBI once kept files on homosexuals?**

Throughout the 1950s, 1960s, and early 1970s, gay and lesbian rights leaders claimed that the FBI was keeping a close eye on their activities. Some people thought this was simply paranoia. It wasn't. According to the late Randy Shilts, a journalist who thoroughly researched internal FBI memorandums, "The FBI conducted exhaustive and apparently illegal surveillance of the gay rights movement and its leaders for more than two decades. The surveillance started in 1953 and was continuing as late as 1975. Agents made extensive use of informants, tape-recorded meetings, collected lists of members of gay organizations, photographed participants in early homosexual rights marches, and investigated advertisers in gay publications."

> **Who are some of the people and what are some of the organizations that have actively worked against the rights of gay and lesbian people and/or spread anti-gay propaganda?**

At the top of my people list are Gary Bauer, James Dobson, Rev. Jerry Falwell, Fred Phelps, Rev. Pat Robertson, and Rev. Lou Sheldon. High on my organization list are the Christian Coalition, the Family Research Council, Focus on the Family, the Southern Baptist Convention, and the Traditional Values Coalition.

18

?

AIDS

› What is AIDS?

AIDS (acquired immunodeficiency syndrome) is a disease of the immune system that, if left untreated, eventually destroys the body's ability to fight other diseases. AIDS is caused by a virus, HIV (human immunodeficiency virus), which can be transmitted when blood, semen, or vaginal secretions containing the virus are passed from one body to another through, for example, unprotected vaginal or anal intercourse, or through intravenous drug use when needles are shared.

I remember being very alarmed by the first article I read in the *New York Times* about forty-one gay men who had been diagnosed with a rare form of cancer. That was in the summer of 1981, and those perplexing cancer cases were just the very beginning of what has become the worldwide AIDS epidemic.

> ### Did gay men cause AIDS?

AIDS is caused by HIV, a virus, not by someone's sexual orientation, and it is spread in a number of ways, not just by one
kind of sexual act.

> ### Is AIDS a gay disease?

AIDS is a human disease that does not distinguish between gay
and nongay people. However, in the United States the epidemic spread first among gay men in major urban areas. Today,
the majority of the millions of AIDS cases worldwide are, by
far, among nongay people.

> ### Do lesbians get AIDS?

Lesbians get AIDS just like everybody else, although female-to-
female transmission of HIV through sex is extremely rare.

> ### How do lesbians get AIDS through sex with other
> ### women?

AIDS is caused by HIV, a virus, which is in the blood, semen,
and vaginal fluids of an infected person. HIV can penetrate
mucous membranes that line the vagina, mouth, and other
parts of the body. So if one woman has the virus, she carries it
in her vaginal fluids. If her sexual partner gets some of these
vaginal fluids in her vagina or mouth, it's possible for her to
become infected with HIV.

> ### If one partner in a male couple has AIDS, won't the
> ### other partner get it?

You can't get AIDS through casual everyday contact with someone who has the disease. So unless the two men do something
that can spread the virus—for example, have anal intercourse
without proper use of a condom or share needles—the HIV-
negative partner will remain free of HIV.

> ### Has AIDS set back the struggle for gay and lesbian equal rights?

At the very beginning of the AIDS epidemic, many gay and lesbian rights activists feared that negative publicity about AIDS would lead to the loss of hard-won rights. But despite their worst fears and the tragic number of deaths from AIDS, including the deaths of many leaders within the gay and lesbian rights movement, AIDS has helped move the gay rights effort in a positive direction in a number of ways.

During the early years of the epidemic, people with AIDS were fired from jobs, evicted from their homes, and denied health insurance, helping throw into sharp focus many of the discrimination issues that gay and lesbian rights leaders had been screaming about for years and very clearly demonstrating the need for laws protecting gay people from discrimination. In addition, AIDS dramatically increased the visibility of gay and lesbian people by putting them in the news almost daily during the height of the AIDS crisis, following years of relative invisibility in the mainstream press. And thousands of gay men and lesbians who had never participated in gay rights efforts were motivated to join the fight against AIDS. Many of these people, who gained extensive experience organizing, fundraising, and working with elected officials, have gone on to work on a variety of gay and lesbian rights issues.

> ### How did AIDS change the public's awareness of gay people?

For years, gay and lesbian rights activists said that if all the gay and lesbian people in the country turned lavender for one day, that would be the end of discrimination against gay people, because all Americans would realize that they knew and loved someone who was gay or lesbian. Though that might not mean the complete end of discrimination, it certainly would shake up a few people and force them to reevaluate their beliefs.

AIDS didn't turn all gay men and lesbians lavender, but with so many gay men dying of the disease in the years before effective treatments became available, AIDS revealed to millions of people—family, friends, colleagues, and neighbors—that they knew and loved someone who was gay, whether that was a cherished brother or a beloved celebrity.

The AIDS epidemic also focused unprecedented media attention on gay and lesbian people. This attention gave those not immediately affected by the AIDS epidemic an opportunity to see that gay men had loving companions, friends, and often supportive families, and that gay and lesbian people were compassionate, hardworking, and courageous people as they organized to spread information about preventing AIDS, took care of the sick and dying, and lobbied for increased spending for AIDS research and swift approval of experimental drugs.

> ### Who are some famous people who were gay and died from AIDS?

Actors Rock Hudson, Anthony Perkins, and Robert Reed (Mike Brady from The Brady Bunch); entertainers Liberace and Peter Allen; attorney Roy Cohn; Washington Redskins tight end Jerry Smith; designer Willi Smith; photographer Robert Mapplethorpe; dancer Rudolf Nureyev; artist Keith Haring; Congressman Stewart McKinney; journalist Randy Shilts; writer Paul Monette—the list goes on and on and on.

> ### Why are gay men still getting infected with HIV when we know how to prevent it?

The better question is, Why are people still getting infected with HIV? Most people become infected with HIV because they fail to do what's necessary to prevent infection. They are not following safer-sex guidelines or are sharing needles during IV drug use.

> ## Why do gay men have unsafe sex?

I had a conversation not long ago with an acquaintance who is very well educated, in the heart of middle age, and a real enthusiast about life. He told me a story about how he had had unprotected anal intercourse with a young man he had just met. My jaw was already on the floor before he got to the part where he told me, "And he ejaculated inside me." I was astonished—no, horrified. "How," I asked, "could you do that?" This man, who has read all the same articles I have and knows people who have died from AIDS, said, "It felt like the right thing to do. I trusted him. He told me that he'd tested negative." Right, and the check is in the mail.

In the heat of passion, people—gay and nongay, young and old—are not always entirely rational, especially when alcohol and/or drugs are part of the mixture. So sometimes even people who know better don't follow safer-sex guidelines. This is especially true of young people, who tend to feel immortal. But besides thinking they'll live forever, many young gay men view AIDS as a disease that belongs to an older generation, and many heterosexuals mistakenly believe that AIDS is a disease that affects only gay men. Also, because younger people most often don't know anyone who has AIDS or has died from AIDS, and think they don't know anyone infected with HIV, they believe they're free from risk of infection.

Other gay men don't follow safer-sex guidelines because they can't acknowledge to themselves that they're gay and engaging in sex with other men, even if that's what they're doing. Because they don't think of themselves as gay, and may mistakenly assume that AIDS is a "gay disease," they think they're not at risk. This kind of thinking may sound far-fetched, but there are many men in very deep denial about who they are and what they're doing. This is an especially acute problem for African-American and Hispanic men, who are even more reluctant than white men to acknowledge that they're gay because of the even more extreme condemnation of homosexuality in their communities.

And finally, some people mistakenly assume that, with more effective treatments available for those infected with HIV, AIDS is no big deal, and not worth the effort of taking proper precautions. But until there's an effective cure for it, AIDS is going to continue to be a big deal.

Whatever the specific reason for not following safer-sex guidelines, gay men—as well as lesbians and nongay people—are only human, and humans do all kinds of things they know are dangerous, like smoking, driving without a seat belt, and drinking too much. Everyone likes to believe, "It won't happen to me." But it can.

> *Where can I get more information on AIDS and safer-sex guidelines?*

Everyone needs to know about AIDS and how to prevent infection with HIV. You can talk to your doctor, call a local health organization, or call a local or national AIDS hot line. The telephone number for the National AIDS Hotline, which is staffed twenty-four hours a day, is 1-800-342-AIDS.

19

?

AGING

> ### Are there old gay and lesbian people?

Of course there are, but when I first found my way into the gay world in New York City in the mid-1970s, my impression was that "old" gay people were around twenty-five or thirty. I rarely saw anyone much older, and I certainly never saw anyone over the age of fifty.

Where were all the older gay and lesbian people? For the most part they were invisible, and many remain so. Gay and lesbian people now in their seventies, eighties, and older grew up in a world that almost uniformly condemned them, a world in which no one spoke of coming out of the closet, because being open about your homosexuality was both unimaginable and dangerous. It's not surprising, then, that, having spent a life in hiding, relatively few of the millions of older gay and lesbian people have come forward. But today, as gay men and lesbians of all ages feel more comfortable with being open, increasing numbers of older gay men and women are making themselves known to their friends, families, and neighbors.

❯ Are there old gay and lesbian couples?

Yes. There are many gay and lesbian couples who have been together for thirty, forty, or fifty years or more. For my book about happy, long-lasting gay and lesbian relationships, I interviewed several older couples, including two women in their eighties who celebrated their fiftieth anniversary in 1998 and two men in their seventies who began their relationship shortly after the end of World War II.

❯ Is it harder growing old if you're gay or lesbian?

Most older gay and lesbian people—men and women in their sixties, seventies, and eighties—are more isolated than their heterosexual counterparts. Most spent their lives hiding their sexual orientation and their relationships, and many plan to take their secret to the grave despite the changes in attitudes in recent decades.

Two older gay and lesbian people I've gotten to know well, Paul and Lina, have shared their secret with only a handful of gay friends, most of whom are now dead. Paul, who is nearly ninety, would like to let the people in his church know that he's gay, but he's afraid they'll think less of him if they know the truth. "I've known I was homosexual since my teens, but I've always felt bad about it," said Paul, who lives by himself in an apartment complex for senior citizens in Denver. "I'd like to say something, but what if they don't accept me? What will I do then?"

Paul told me that he would like to find a companion, "not for a physical relationship—I can't do that anymore—but for the company." He asked me, "Do you think it's too late for me to meet someone?" Given how fearful Paul was of revealing the truth about his orientation, I didn't think it was likely, but I told him I thought there was always a possibility.

Lina, who is nearly eighty, lives in a small bungalow just outside Seattle with her two dogs and four cats. Only the two "gay boys" who live across the street from her know that she's a lesbian. "I think they knew I was gay soon after they moved in. I still haven't asked them how they could tell. We've gotten friendly over the past few years, and now we always share articles and books that talk about gays. Last week they drove me to the vet. One of the dogs was sick. I'm lucky to have them. They tell me they're lucky to have me."

For some gay and lesbian people, the sense of isolation can be extreme. They may have shared their secret with only one person—a long-term partner, for example. After the death of that partner, these men and women have no one with whom to share their lives and reminiscences and no one with whom they can be completely honest.

But isolation, while common, isn't everyone's experience. The two half-century couples I interviewed for my long-term couples book are very visible in their respective communities in Delaware and Florida. While you're not likely to find them holding hands on the street, both couples make no effort to hide their relationships. Shortly before I met them, the two women were featured in their local newspaper and the two men were called onstage during a public commitment ceremony for two hundred gay and lesbian couples at their church. When introduced to the assembled crowd, they were greeted with enthusiastic cheers.

Old age means all kinds of challenges for all men and women, but for gay people there's the added challenge of dealing with social service agencies and health care providers that may have no experience with gay men and lesbians. This can be especially difficult for couples, who may be reluctant to reveal the relationship they have with their "best friend" or "housemate." Imagine, for example, the challenge faced by a woman who needs to find a nursing home for her long-term partner who is suffering from severe memory loss, but doesn't want to reveal that they are more than just roommates. Because she and her beloved are just close friends—as far as the nursing home knows—they will be treated very differently from a heterosexual married couple. And unless she and her partner have completed the necessary legal documents, the healthy partner will not be able to make medical and financial decisions for her ill spouse.

> ### Are there organizations for older gay and lesbian people?

There are organizations for gay and lesbian senior citizens in most major cities. The oldest and best-known organization, SAGE—Senior Action in a Gay Environment—is located in New York City. Working primarily with residents in the New York area, it provides a range of services to elderly gay men and lesbians, including home, hospital, and institutional visiting, transportation to doctors, weekly workshops and discussion groups, and monthly parties. SAGE also acts as a go-between for clients and government agencies, landlords, and hospitals. It also helps people find retirement homes that welcome gay and lesbian people. (See "Resources" for listing.)

> ### Are there retirement homes specifically for gay people?

Although retirement homes specifically for gay and lesbian senior citizens don't yet exist, many care providers are beginning to address the fact that not all senior citizens are heterosexual.

One social worker I spoke with, who works with nursing homes to make them aware of the special needs of gay and lesbian residents, told me that most nursing homes have a very long way to go before they deal realistically with the issue of homosexuality.

While no retirement homes for gay and lesbian people currently exist (as of early 1999), SAGE in New York City has been actively involved in investigating the feasibility of such a project.

> ### What do grandchildren think of their gay grandparents?

Some people have trouble adjusting to the idea that Grandma is a lesbian or Grandpa is gay. And others love their grandparents just the same.

In an interview in the New York Times several years ago, a seventy-nine-year-old woman, who asked to be identified as Gerry, said that when she told her daughter about her secret life, her daughter told her grandchildren, "Grandma's gay." According to the interview, "Gerry said that the kids looked at their mother and remarked, 'So what else is new?' Gerry smiled and said, 'It made me feel like I was only seventy years old.'"

> ### Do gay people take care of elderly parents?

There are no statistics on the number of gay and lesbian people who are taking care of elderly parents, but plenty do it.

Jim and Lane, who live in rural North Carolina, are just one example. They took care of Lane's elderly mother for the last dozen years of her life. Lane told me: "She's got all these children—I'm one of nine—and nobody else would help her." Jim and Lane did everything for Lane's mother, from helping her bathe to getting her to the doctor and watching over her medicines. When her memory began to fail and she couldn't be left at home alone, the two men began taking Lane's mother with them to work. Jim and Lane run a carpet cleaning and dyeing business.

Jim told me: "We couldn't get anyone to stay with her, and we didn't have the money to pay for anybody to stay with her. Everything we did has been out of necessity. You do what you have to do when you ain't got the money to do it. You make the best of it and improvise. So we had a van, which Lane remodeled. He put in captain's chairs, and he put a window in the side and installed an RV bathroom. Every morning we'd walk Mom up the ramp into the back of the van, and she'd go to Charlotte with us to clean carpets. We brought along our dog and our cat, and the cat would sit on her lap all day. We did that for about two years, and Mom loved it. She had her picture window right by her seat, and she'd watch everything going on. And a lot of people at the apartment complexes got to know her, and they'd come and visit with her out at the truck. When the weather was pretty, we'd take lawn chairs with us, and when we were doing a job, we'd put the lawn chairs out and let Mom sit in the yard. She liked the routine, and it got her out of the house."

20

—

?

MORE QUESTIONS . . .

> *What is a transgendered person?*
> *What is a transsexual?*

These words are moving targets, and it seems that no two people I spoke with could agree on exactly what they meant. So I turned to someone who works with transgendered/transsexual youth at a group home in New York City. What follows is a paraphrase of what he told me.

Transgender is an umbrella term that covers a broad range of "gender expression" including drag queens and kings (see the next page), bigenders, cross-dressers, transgenderists, and transsexuals. These individuals are often people who find their gender identity—the sense of themselves as male or female—in conflict with their anatomical gender.

Transsexuals are people who have a gender identity disorder. Some, although not all, transsexuals feel as though they are trapped in the wrong body. In other words, a man may feel he belongs in a woman's body. And a woman may feel she belongs in a man's body. Some transsexuals may live part-time in their self-defined gender, dressing and behaving in a manner generally associated with that gender, and others choose to live full-time in their self-identified gender. Some transsexuals also decide to undergo sexual reassignment surgery.

> **What is a transvestite?**
> **Are all transvestites gay men?**
> **What is a drag queen?**
> **What is a drag king?**

People use the word *transvestite* and the phrase *drag queen* to mean all kinds of different things, whether it's in reference to a gay man who likes to dress up in women's clothing for weekend parties or someone who dresses up in women's clothing and performs onstage. Here are my official definitions based on my research.

A transvestite is someone who dresses in the clothing of the opposite gender and for whom that dressing is sexually exciting. Most transvestites are heterosexual men, and they do their cross-dressing in secret or only in the company of other heterosexual transvestites.

People who dress up in clothing of the opposite gender for a costume party, for a play, or just because they like doing it are said to be "cross-dressing" or dressing in "drag." A gay man who does this is sometimes called a *drag queen*. A lesbian who does this is sometimes called a *drag king*. A man who dresses as a woman to perform professionally in public is called a *female impersonator*.

› *What is a drag ball?*

Many people have gotten a close look at one type of drag ball in Jennie Livingston's remarkable award-winning 1991 documentary film, Paris Is Burning (well worth renting if you can get your hands on a copy). In it, Livingston introduced viewers to Harlem drag balls, where African-American and Hispanic gay men and women dress up to compete for trophies in different categories. In the "Realness" category, for example, gay men try to "pass" as heterosexual schoolboys, executives, street thugs, soldiers, and beautiful, glamorous women.

Another type of drag ball is held in the context of the Imperial Court System, which is one of the oldest and largest gay charitable organizations. Dating back to the early 1960s, the several dozen individual "courts" of the Imperial Court System around the country hold fund-raising balls to benefit both local and national gay, as well as nongay, charities. People who attend these balls, primarily gay men, dress in all kinds of formal attire. For example, the instruction booklet for the high camp "Night of a Thousand Gowns" charity ball held at the Waldorf-Astoria Hotel by the Imperial Court of New York states: "Full court dress is preferred: elegant gowns with tiaras, orders, and family jewels, and/or white tie and tails (knee breeches with silver buckles, for those with the legs for it). Black tie is acceptable, though there is always the possibility of your being mistaken for a waiter. Military personnel may wear dress uniform with full regimentals; swords are optional (but dueling is prohibited)."

› *What is a drag show?*

A drag show is just what it sounds like. It's a show—whether it takes place on the floor of a gay dance club or on a Broadway stage—that features female impersonators. Typically the show involves impersonating a famous actress or performer, or inventing an entirely fictional character. There's usually lots of makeup, big hair, very high heels, and sequins. The performance can range from a comedy stand-up routine or lip-synching a variety of songs to a full-length one-"woman" show based on the life of the celebrity being impersonated.

> *Why do some gay people dress up in black leather?*

Sometimes gay and lesbian people, just like heterosexual people, wear black leather garments—pants, jacket, boots, and so on—simply because they like to wear black leather. It may be nothing more than a fashion statement. For other gay and lesbian people—and nongay people—black leather garments and accessories are an indication that they engage in S&M (sadism and masochism) role-playing and/or sex. Their black leather garments are part of a uniform that is recognized by other people who are a part of the "leather community." (However, not all people who engage in S&M dress in black leather.)

> *How do countries outside the United States deal with gay and lesbian people?*

Around the world, the situation for gay and lesbian people varies by country and region. In general, European countries have very liberal attitudes toward homosexuality. Even in Russia, where sodomy laws were used from the 1930s until 1993 to send gay men to Siberian work camps, gay men and women are now free from official sanctions, although they remain a generally scorned minority.

In other parts of the world, particularly Asia and Africa, gay and lesbian people face enormous oppression and even fear for their lives. In Iran, for example, homosexual acts are illegal for both men and women and are punishable by death. In Zimbabwe, President Robert Mugabe has led a very public antigay campaign, calling gay and lesbian people "worse than pigs and dogs," declaring that they had no civil rights (as of early 1999). In contrast, South Africa's constitution bans "unfair" discrimination on the basis of sexual orientation, although gay couples there are still forbidden by law to adopt.

Many countries have no laws that forbid homosexual relations, but that doesn't mean gay and lesbian people can lead their lives in a climate free from prejudice or harm. In China, homosexuals are sometimes treated for what most doctors there consider a mental illness. Two of the most popular methods used in China to "cure" homosexuality, according to a story published in the *New York Times*, are meant to discourage erotic thoughts through the application of painful electric shocks or induced vomiting. On the bright side, the article goes on to note that though most Chinese frown on homosexuality, it is considered in poor taste or improper rather than sinful. There are also "no common insults in Chinese related to sexual orientation."

I correspond regularly with a young gay man in central China, and while he's never been forced to undergo treatment for his sexual orientation, he said that he can never live his life openly or even hope to enter into a couple relationship. He fears that unless he leaves China, he will be left with little choice but to marry a woman and pretend to be heterosexual.

> **Are there as many gay people in other countries as there are in the United States?**

The same percentage of people the world over have feelings of attraction for those of the same gender. The primary differences are in how people choose to express—or not express—these feelings, and how various governments and cultures choose to deal with gay and lesbian people.

> **Can gay and lesbian people from countries outside the United States become U.S. citizens?**

Until 1990, federal law barred people "with psychopathic personality, or sexual deviation, or a mental defect" from even en-

tering the United States. This law was used to bar entry of homosexual aliens, and it was upheld in 1967, when the U.S.
Supreme Court ruled that homosexuals could be barred from
the country as sexual deviants.

In November 1990, President George Bush signed into law
an immigration reform bill that included the elimination of
restrictions based on sexual orientation.

> ### Why do some gay people have piercings and tattoos?

During the 1990s, piercings—pierced ears, noses, nipples, lips,
eyebrows, you name it—and tattoos became increasingly popular, particularly among both gay and nongay adolescents and
young adults.

People who choose to be pierced and/or adorn their bodies with tattoos do so for various reasons. Some people do it as
a fashion or political statement. Others do it to fit in with a
peer or social group. And still others get pierced and tattooed
to rebel against their parents.

One young man I talked to, who has several tattoos, said
that by marking his body, "I can express my individuality in a
way I can't with clothes or a haircut." A woman I spoke with
agreed, adding that her tattoos and piercings showed her "tribal
allegiance." "Between my clothes, haircut, tattoos, and piercings, I get my point across that I'm a member of the tribe."

> ### Are gay men more sensitive than nongay men?

Some gay men are sensitive and understanding. And so are
some nongay men. But are gay men inherently more sensitive
and understanding than heterosexual men?

One theory I've heard over the years is that gay men are in
general more sensitive than nongay men because the experience of growing up gay—being an outsider—and having to
examine their lives and come to terms with something that

makes them different from others gives many gay men more insight about life, making them more sensitive than the average heterosexual man to the challenges faced by other people. It's a nice theory, and I even think it has some merit, but there are still plenty of gay men who are insensitive blockheads.

> **Why are so many gay men fans of opera?**

There is a disproportionate number of gay men who can't resist the call of opera. To me it's something of a mystery. I can't get through La Bohème without falling asleep during the third act. And with Janácek's Katia Kabanova, I couldn't make it through the first act, and that despite the fact that I flew to Chicago to hear a friend who was singing a leading role in it. Fortunately, she didn't glance down into the front row—she had gotten us house seats—to see me with my head slumped over. But I'm exaggerating. I've really enjoyed seeing Madame Butterfly and loved Patience & Sarah, a lesbian opera that premiered in 1998 at the Lincoln Center Summer Festival in New York City.

I asked one of my oldest friends, who has been a opera aficionado since college—though not a true opera queen, he would say—what he thought opera's attraction was for gay men. He told me: "Opera aficionados can be of any gender or orientation. These are people who feel a deep connection with the drama, the music, and the spectacle. Opera queens, on the other hand, are focused on opera divas. They're there for the lead female singer. They are not interested in what else occurs on the stage, except perhaps for the rare attractive tenor over five feet tall. What they love about the divas is their combination of strength and vulnerability, but the crux of the opera queen's obsession is that the diva is bigger than life. They are watching someone act out on a ridiculously vast scale emotions that they can't begin to imagine acting out in their own lives.

"I think the classic opera queen is becoming less of a type as more men are able to lead openly gay lives. In the 1950s and '60s opera queens were typically men who had relatively dull lives and were uniformly closeted. Then in the dark of the theater they could completely fantasize and thrill to the fabulous icon of the opera diva. This sounds terrible to say, almost homophobic, but I think it was largely true of earlier generations of gay men who were forced to live such circumscribed lives. Opera gave them the opportunity to escape, and that's still one of the reasons all kinds of people enjoy opera."

My opera friend pointed out that there's even a subcategory of opera queens who are "high-note queens." These are gay men who, he explained, live solely for the auditory thrill of high notes produced by divas, whom they worship for their ability to sing such notes.

If you would like a book-length answer to the questions of why so many gay men love opera and what makes an "opera queen," I recommend reading *The Queen's Throat: Opera, Homosexuality, and the Mystery of Desire* by Wayne Koestenbaum.

> ### Why do some women performers attract a large gay male following?

After posing this question to several people, both gay and nongay, I found that the only thing they could agree on was that people such as Judy Garland, Joan Crawford, Barbra Streisand, Bette Midler, Bette Davis, Marilyn Monroe, and Liza Minnelli were popular with an apparently large number of gay men. Several offered the explanation that the gay men who are fans of these women are attracted to the combined strength and vulnerability these women have projected in their work.

I thought that the best explanation came from a man who wrote to me from Maryland in response to my request for help in answering this question in this book's original edition. He wrote: "In the case of Judy Garland and Marilyn Monroe, I think a lot of gay men can identify with their legendary reputations for suffering, combined with their vulnerability and their bad luck with both spouses and management. We identify with Streisand for very different reasons: She is seen as a powerful, hard-working survivor who attacked and beat the odds against her, when no one could imagine anyone with such off-beat looks and personality finding success as a performer.

"Bette Davis and Joan Crawford were equally strong and hard-headed, but many of the characters they played in films could be looked at as fictional counterparts to the real lives of Garland and Monroe: suffering victims destined to lose, frequently played to the hilt of camp sensibility. And we love Liza partly because we celebrate her success at picking up where her mother left off, and partly because she suffered similar setbacks. . . . Of course, it doesn't hurt that these women are also massively talented and [compelling]."

> **Do gay people have an impact on popular culture?**

Gay and lesbian people have long had a major influence on popular culture, from the clothes we wear and the advertisements we see to the kind of music we dance to and the stories we read.

I like what the writer Fran Lebowitz has said on this subject: "If you removed all the homosexuals and homosexual influence from what is generally regarded as American culture, you would be pretty much left with *Let's Make a Deal.*"

BIBLIOGRAPHY

Aarons, Leroy. *Prayers for Bobby: A Mother's Coming to Terms with the Suicide of Her Gay Son.* San Francisco: Harper San Francisco, 1996.

The Alyson Almanac: The Gay and Lesbian Fact Book. Boston: Alyson Publications, 1997.

Bérubé, Allan. *Coming Out Under Fire: The History of Gay Men and Women in World War Two.* New York: Plume, 1991.

Berzon, Betty. *The Intimacy Dance: A Guide to Long-Term Success in Gay and Lesbian Relationships.* New York: Plume, 1997.

————. *Permanent Partners: Building Gay and Lesbian Relationships That Last.* New York: Plume, 1990.

————, ed. *Positively Gay: New Approaches to Gay and Lesbian Life.* Berkeley, CA: Celestial Arts, 1992.

Borhek, Mary V. *Coming Out to Parents: A Two-Way Survival Guide for Lesbians and Gay Men and Their Parents.* New York: Pilgrim Press, 1993.

————. *My Son Eric: A Mother Struggles to Accept Her Gay Son and Discovers Herself.* New York: Pilgrim Press, 1984.

Boswell, John. *Christianity, Social Tolerance, and Homosexuality: Gay People in Western Europe from the Beginning of the Christian Era to the Fourteenth Century.* Chicago: Univ. of Chicago Press, 19801.

Bright, Susie. *Susie Sexpert's Lesbian Sex World.* Pittsburgh: Cleis Press, 1999.

Browning, Frank. *The Culture of Desire: Paradox and Perversity in Gay Lives Today.* New York: Vintage Books, 1994.

Bruni, Frank, Elinor Burkett. *A Gospel of Shame: Children, Sexual Abuse and the Catholic Church.* New York: Viking, 1993.

Burr, Chandler, Rick Kot (Editor). *A Separate Creation: The Search for the Biological Origins of Sexual Orientation.* New York: Hyperion, 1997.

Buxton, Amity Pierce. *The Other Side of the Closet: The Coming-Out Crisis for Straight Spouses.* New York: John Wiley & Sons, 1994.

Curry, Hayden, and Denis Clifford. *A Legal Guide for Lesbian and Gay Couples.* Berkeley, CA: Nolo Press, 1999.

D'Emilio, John. *Sexual Politics, Sexual Communities: The Making of a Homosexual Minority in the United States, 1940–1970.* Chicago: Univ. of Chicago Press, 1998.

Faderman, Lillian. *Odd Girls and Twilight Lovers: A History of Lesbian Life in Twentieth-Century America.* New York: Penguin USA, 1992.

Fairchild, Betty, and Nancy Hayward. Now That You Know: A Parent's Guide to Understanding Their Gay and Lesbian Children. New York: Harcourt Brace Jovanovich, 1998.

Fricke, Aaron. Reflections of a Rock Lobster: A Story About Growing Up Gay. St. Paul: Consortium Book Sales & Distribution, 1995.

Griffin, Carolyn Welch, Marian J. Wirth, and Arthur G. Wirth. Beyond Acceptance: Parents of Lesbians and Gays Talk About Their Experiences. New York: St. Martin's Press, 1997.

Heger, Heinz. Men with the Pink Triangle: The True, Life-and-Death Story of Homosexuals in the Nazi Death Camps. Boston: Alyson Publications, 1994.

Helminiak, Daniel A., Ph.D., What the Bible Really Says About Homosexuality. San Francisco: Alamo Square Press, 1994.

Herek, Gregory M. Hate Crimes: Confronting Violence Against Lesbians and Gay Men. Newbury Park, CA: Sage Publications, 1991.

Heron, Ann. Two Teenagers in Twenty: Writings by Gay and Lesbian Youth. Boston: Alyson Publications, 1995.

Hunter, Nan D., Sherryl E. Michaelson, and Thomas B. Stoddard. The Rights of Lesbians and Gay Men: The Basic ACLU Guide to Gay Person's Rights. 3d ed. Carbondale: Southern Illinois Univ. Press, 1992.

Hutchings, Loraine, and Lani Kaahumanu. Bi Any Other Name: Bisexual People Speak Out. Boston: Alyson Publications, 1991.

Koestenbaum, Wayne. The Queen's Throat: Opera, Homosexuality, and the Mystery of Desire. New York: Vintage Books, 1994.

Kopay, David, and Perry Deane Young. The David Kopay Story. New York: Donald I. Fine, 1988.

Laumann, Edward O., Robert T. Michael (Editor), John H. Gagnon, Stuart Michaels (Editor). The Social Organization of Sexuality: Sexual Practices in the United States. Chicago: Univ. of Chicago Press, 1994.

Lewin, Ellen. Recognizing Ourselves: Ceremonies of Lesbian and Gay Commitment (Between Men—Between Women). New York: Columbia University Press, 1998.

Marcus, Eric. Making History: The Struggle for Gay and Lesbian Equal Rights, 1945–1990. New York: Harper Collins, 1992.

————. The Male Couple's Guide: Finding a Man, Making a Home, Building a Life. New York: Harper Collins, 1999.

————. Together Forever: Gay and Lesbian Couples Share Their Secrets for Lasting Happiness. New York: Anchor, 1999.

Martin, April. *The Lesbian and Gay Parenting Handbook: Creating and Raising Our Families.* New York: Harper Collins, 1993.

McNaught, Brian. *Gay Issues in the Workplace.* New York: St. Martin's Press, 1995.

———. *Now That I'm Out, What Do I Do?* New York: St. Martin's Press, 1998.

McNeill, John J. *The Church and the Homosexual.* New York: Beacon Press, 1993.

Miller, Neil. *Out in the World: Gay and Lesbian Life from Buenos Aires to Bangkok.* New York: Vintage Books, 1993.

Pies, Cheri. *Considering Parenthood.* San Francisco: Spinsters, 1988.

Plant, Richard. *The Pink Triangle: The Nazi War Against Homosexuals.* New York: Henry Holt and Company, 1988.

Russo, Vito. *The Celluloid Closet: Homosexuality in the Movies.* New York: Harper Collins, 1987.

Scanzoni, Letha Dawson, and Virginia Ramey Mollenkott. *Is the Homosexual My Neighbor?: A Positive Christian Response.* Rev. ed. San Francisco: HarperSanFrancisco, 1994.

Schow, Ron, Wayne Schow, and Marybeth Raynes. *Peculiar People: Mormons and Same-Sex Orientation.* Salt Lake City: Signature Books, 1993.

Schulenburg, Joy A. *Gay Parenting: A Complete Guide for Gay Men and Lesbians with Children.* Garden City, NY: Anchor Press, 1985.

Shilts, Randy. *And the Band Played On: Politics, People, and the AIDS Epidemic.* New York: Penguin USA, 1995.

———. *Conduct Unbecoming: Gays and Lesbians in the U.S. Military.* New York: St. Martin's Press, 1993.

Spong, John Shelby. *Living in Sin? A Bishop Rethinks Human Sexuality.* San Francisco: HarperSanFrancisco, 1990.

Vacha, Keith. *Quiet Fire: Memoirs of Older Gay Men.* Trumansburg, NY: Crossing Press, 1985.

Van Gelder, Lindsy, and Pamela Robin Brandt. *Are You Two . . . Together? A Gay and Lesbian Travel Guide to Europe.* New York: Random House, 1991.

———. *The Girls Next Door: Into the Heart of Lesbian America.* New York: Fireside, 1997.

Witt, Lynn (Editor), Sherry Thomas (Editor), Eric Marcus (Editor). *Out in All Directions: A Treasury of Gay and Lesbian America.* New York: Warner Books, 1997.

RESOURCES

COLAGE (Children of Lesbians and Gays Everywhere)
tel.: 415–861–5437
Web site: www.colage.org
e-mail: colage@colage.org

The Family Pride Coalition
tel.: 619–296–0199
Web site: www.familypride.org
e-mail: pride@familypride.org

GLAAD (Gay and Lesbian Alliance Against Defamation)
150 West 26th St., #503
New York, NY 10001
tel.: 212–807–1700
Web site: www.glaad.org

GLSEN (Gay, Lesbian & Straight Education Network)
121 West 27th St., #804
New York, NY 10001
tel.: 212–727–0135
Web site: www.glsen.org
e-mail: glsen@glsen.org

**HRC
Human Rights Campaign**
1101 14th St., NW, #800
Washington, DC 20005
tel.: 202–628–4160
Web site: www.hrc.org
e-mail: info@hrc.org

Lambda Legal Defense and Education Fund
120 Wall St., #1500
New York, NY 10005
tel.: 212–809–8585
Web site: www.lambdalegal.org

National AIDS Hotline
800–342-AIDS

New York City Gay and Lesbian Anti-Violence Project
240 West 35th St., #200
New York, NY 10001
tel.: 212–714–1141
Web site: www.avp.org

NGLTF (National Gay and Lesbian Task Force)
2320 17th St., N.W.
Washington, DC 20009–2702
tel.: 202–332–6483
Web site: www.ngltf.org
e-mail: ngltf@ngltf.org

NLGJA (National Lesbian & Gay Journalists Association)
1718 M St., NW, #245
Washington, DC 20036
tel.: 202–588–9888
Web site: www.nlgja.org
e-mail: nlgja@aol.com

NYAC (National Youth Advocacy Coalition)
1711 Connecticut Ave., NW, #206
Washington, DC 20009
tel.: 202–319–7596
Web site: www.nyacyouth.org
e-mail: nyac@nyacyouth.org

PFLAG (Parents, Families and Friends of Lesbians and Gays)
1101 14th St., N.W., #1030
Washington, DC 20005
tel.: 202–638–4200
Web site: www.pflag.org
e-mail: info@pflag.org

SAGE (Senior Action in a Gay Environment)
305 7th Avenue
New York, NY 10001
tel.: 212–741–2247
e-mail: sageusa@aol.com

SLDN (Servicemembers Legal Defense Network)
PO Box 65301
Washington, DC 20035
tel.: 202–328–3244
Web site: www.sldn.com
e-mail: sldn@sldn.org

INDEX